To

Stay blessed

Homeless Lives Matter!

To Julie
Stay blessed

Homeless Lives Matter!

Homeless my story

Leo Gnawa

Cabri Mort Media

Copyright © 2016 Leo Gnawa

First edition

ISBN-13:
978-1523731374

ISBN-10:

1523731370

SPECIAL DEDICATION:

TO ALL THOSE WHO HAVE SHOWN ME COMPASSION

TABLE OF CONTENTS

PAGES:

Introduction

I was sitting on the steps of an abandoned building on the corner of 13th and G Streets in Northwest Washington DC, about three short blocks from the White House. I was approached by a white man who was about 40 years old or maybe a little younger. He asked me if I had seen an old white homeless man who hangs around the area every morning. I answered no. "I told him that I would bring him a winter coat here tonight when I saw him on my way to work this morning," he said, while holding a brand new jacket. I suggested to him, to check inside the entrance of the bank down the block, because I used to see a homeless man sleep there by the cash machine at night. "I parked my car here, but I will walk there and check," he responded. He returned about 15 minutes later and told me that he checked inside the bank entrance, and walked around the block, unsuccessfully.

He did not look too happy. I wouldn't either if I was him. It was a very cold winter, and this kind and generous man who lives far in Virginia, could have just drove home after work and attend to his personal affairs, like everybody else. But instead, he went to a store, purchased a brand new jacket and drove back to the city, only to find out that the needy man he did all this for, did not show up at the location where they had agreed to meet.

Are you homeless?" He asked me. "Yes," I responded. "I know this jacket is not quite your size, but you may be able to fit it. You can have it if you need it," he said to me. "I doubt I can fit it," I told him. The jacket was size XL, therefore I could barely fit it because I normally wear size XXL at least.

"You need a jacket? I can bring you one next time, if you do," he said. I could not turn down such an offer because I did not have a thick enough jacket for the winter. But before I gave him an answer, he asked me, "Why are you homeless? I want to hear your story." Because he seemed genuine enough in his compassion and charity, I agreed to explain to him why I was Homeless.

He spent the following 30 minutes listening to my story and asked me what I needed, and when and where to meet me next time. He brought me a brand new jacket at Martin Luther King Library on a Saturday afternoon, a couple of days later. I used to go there to work on my laptop, charge its battery, access the Library's WIFI, and warm up indoors, after spending the night sleeping outside in the cold.

Since then, he had checked on me from time to time, encouraged, uplifted and helped me in so many ways. I dedicated the book to him, because he suggested and insisted that I write a book about my homeless story, since I had confided to him that I had a passion for writing and had, few years ago, written some articles, several times, in Street Sense, which is a local homeless newspaper. I also wanted to express my gratitude to him for his compassion and generosity towards me. But, to be honest, at first, I resented the idea of exposing my homeless reality publicly, although I had already started writing another book related to my political activism on international human rights and democracy advocacy. As a political activist, I have been discreet about my homelessness and never exposed it to the folks, with whom I have organized and interacted at, public events, protests and activities locally.

I have never been comfortable about divulging my homelessness to people unless they were already aware of it. Homelessness to me is disgraceful and embarrassing. So how could I write a book to reveal to the whole wide world that I am a homeless? It was not an easy thing to do, but I overcame my initial reluctance and decided to do it, after I seriously pondered on how beneficial to me writing a book on my homelessness would be after all.

Initially, I followed the advice of the Good Samaritan who suggested that I used a penname to write the book without exposing my real identity. But, first I thought about using the penname Leo Johnson, which is an alias that I have used as my homeless name, when I did not want to expose my real name in my homeless environment. But, at the last minute, I decided to use my real name instead, because after all, this is my real story and I can't hide it forever. So, I don't care who knows whether I am or have been homeless or not. To make it brief, this is how the idea to write this book came about. It is by no means my intention to make a case that, it is ok for me or anyone to be homeless. If I ever came across as suggesting so, please, I ask you to forgive me. I can assure you that I understand very clearly that, being homeless is dehumanizing, and it is imperative for me or anyone else in that situation, to try our very best to remove ourselves from homelessness.

My only and sincere objective here is to provide answers to the questions that I am constantly asked, which are: Why am I homeless? How do I survive as homeless? What did I experience as homeless? How do I feel about being homeless and homelessness in general from my own experience? What am I doing or have I done to come out of homelessness? In addition to providing answers to these questions, I also urged people to be compassionate to the homeless and not despise them. As a matter of fact, I also talked about how I have seen society and people mistreat and take advantage of the homeless. I concluded the book by expressing, what I think can be done to end homelessness. So dear reader, I sincerely want to express my gratitude to you for reading this book. I hope that it will help you have a better understanding of the social plague called homelessness.

CHAPTER 1

THE HOMELESS ARE HUMAN BEINGS LIKE YOU

PUT YOURSELF IN THE SHOES OF A HOMELESS PERSON:

It is so unfortunate to notice the apathy for the homeless on the streets by the majority of people, who walk pass them, from dawn to dusk and dusk to dawn, every day and night. I can only guess that, one of the reasons of that is because most people cannot relate to what the homeless go through, because they are not trying -at least sometimes- to put themselves in their shoes. I can admit myself that, how I feel about the homeless today is far different from how I felt about the homeless then. Before the day that I got evicted for the first time twenty two years ago, I could have never imagined that I would one day be homeless. But here I am in January 2016 and still homeless off and on since 2003.

I remember the eve of the night that I was to be evicted from the very first time; it was dreadful. I had nowhere to go. I became depressed and entertained suicidal thoughts, because of the anxiety that the thought that I was about to become homeless for the first time in my life caused me. I got out of my apartment and took a walk to a payphone a block away. Cell phones were unheard of then, and payphones were still available on street corners, unlike nowadays. I called the suicide hotline. I talked to the person on the other side of the line but became uncomfortable with the conversation and simply hung up the phone. I had realized that I was just overacting. So, I walked back to my apartment and tried to enjoy the last good sleep and night there. I got up early in the morning to figure out what to do with my belongings. I had no other option but take my important documents and a backpack with few clothes and simply abandon all my belongings inside the apartment. Then I walked away.

THE KIDS WHO LAUGHED AT ME:

Here is a story which illustrates the general apathy many homeless experience daily from their fellow human beings, who are neither capable of putting themselves in their shoes, nor able to imagine that they could themselves be homeless.

I had left let my tent, made a stop at the soup kitchen at SOME House where I had lunch, then walked from there on my way to the small branch of the DC library. It is near the Sumsum Corda low-income housing complex and neighborhood, in North West Washington DC.

I was walking not too far behind a man when I saw a group of small school kids throw rocks at him behind his back, as he walked pass the playground of the RH Terrell recreational center, which is contiguous to the Northwest One Library. Most of them were black girls of about the ages of 9 to 11, and likely, residents of the Sumsum Corda housing complex. I kept my eyes on them because I anticipated that they would do the same to me as soon as I have my back turned, when I walk pass the fenced playground where they were playing in their school uniforms.

They held rocks in their hands and advanced towards the fence as a pack of wolves towards their prey. A couple of them uttered slurs like, "Hey you boy! I will punch you in the face, boy!" I was so shocked to watch these little 8 to

10 year old girls call a 50 year old man like me, a boy, and think that it was cute to joke around, by disrespecting folks who could be older than their parents.

"I am old enough to be your father, and you have to respect people old enough to be your parents," I told the most aggressive of them who was running to the fence with a rock in her hand. Then another one, who noticed the big navy backpack that I was carrying on my back and also my not-so-well-kept appearance, howled "He got a big bag on his back, He is homeless." The rest of them followed suit and hollered; "You homeless! He homeless." I felt humiliated by their verbal assault, and wondered whether I would have felt so much hurt if I had just let them lapidate me.

I was baffled and chagrined by the insensitivity of these black kids towards an older black homeless man like me, although they probably live in a low-income neighborhood and their parents were likely poor also.

"You may end up becoming homeless yourself" I told the most aggressive one. "No, I will never be homeless." She retorted emotionally, while holding her hips with both hands and moving her head from left to right while leaning her torso forward. "How you know that? Don't laugh at the homeless, but pray that you do not become homeless when you grow up," I kept on scolding her.

I was very surprised that no teacher was around to witness this interaction, although one of the child had initially said, "we are not supposed to talk to strangers."

But I felt relieved when I reached the end the fence safely, although, the conversation I initiated with these kids to distract and deter them from lapidating me was hurtful, because they laughed at me for being homeless. If these kids had thought for one second, that they too could be homeless, I am certain that they would have expressed empathy instead of derision towards me.

IMAGINE YOURSELF HOMELESS:

Before I start, I want to assure you that if you care for the homeless, what I am about to say here does not concern you. So, please do not take offense if you sense anger in my tone, because I am truly expressing the anger that many homeless feel when they are being ignored by the hundreds of people who walk pass them and seem not to notice their presence. But if you are one of those who, for whatever reasons, do not feel the need to show empathy to the homeless, I do respect your opinion and feelings. Most likely, you have your own relevant personal, philosophical and ideological justifications, and it is not my place to cast judgment on you. I know you also have your own issues that you may be focused on and cannot focus on somebody else issues. That is very understandable. So, I am by no means trying to malign you for not making of somebody else problem, your problem. That will not be fair to you. My aim here is to try to get you to have compassion for the homeless, by simply putting yourself in their shoes and imagining how you would like others to have sympathy for you. For example, I want you to think for a minute that you were being evicted of your home and had nowhere else to move in.

Imagine yourself being a homeless who had to spend his or her days outdoors or in public places and was denied access to a public restroom at a hotel nearby or at Mac Donald down the street. And, you can't urinate or defecate outside for fear of being arrested by the police if you were caught.

Guess for a moment that people avoid sitting next to you on the bus or on the train, or security officers follow you inside stores because they suspect you to be inside there to steal simply because you look homeless. I can go on and on, but just think of these few scenarios, and I bet you will feel terrified by the thought of you having to go through these tribulations as a homeless on the streets. I can tell you without a shadow of a doubt that, being homeless is not easy. It is shameful, dehumanizing, distressing, perilous and I can go on and on with the negatives; and I speak from my own experience and not what somebody else told me.

I have seen homeless people degenerate into some mental illnesses, because they did not cope very well with the hardship and stress of homelessness. I myself, had always been concerned about my mental health to the point that, I prayed one day to God -whoever that is- to take everything from me but not touch my sanity.

Even a person who is perfectly mentally healthy can end up losing his or her mind, if he or she does not cope well enough with the reality of homelessness. So whenever you see a homeless man or woman, understand that you are coming across a person who is suffering a lot emotionally, mentally and physically.

Do not be surprised when you see so many homeless men and women who are mentally ill or suffering from some kind of mental condition or at least some severe depression. Do not be surprised also to see many homeless addicted to drug and alcohol, because in reality many of them use drugs and alcohol to escape from their misery or also to self-medicate.

Any and every homeless person, male or female, child, adult or elderly, deserves the respect of his dignity as anybody else, whatever his or her condition, state of mind or weaknesses; whether self-inflicted or the result of a situation beyond his or her control.

Imagine how the homeless feel when the majority of the hundreds of pedestrians who walk pass them on the street every day, simply ignore and pretend that they do not see or hear them as if the homeless were invisible. Some people simply despise the homeless and feel so offended when they beg them for money. But think about it for a minute! If you were an indigent person who was sleeping on a street sidewalk by a building in the city's downtown area, wouldn't you want anybody to offer you some money whether you beg for it or not? So why be so offended because somebody who has nothing asks you for some change or some food?

Even if you can't give the homeless beggar some money, at least acknowledge his humanity and say something to him or her, like "sorry! I don't have any money". Your response may be a lie, but at least you have not ignored them, no matter what their reaction may be. Off course, you cannot help every homeless who begs you for help at each street corner every day, otherwise you would end up penniless and homeless yourself. But you can always help, at least, one person with a little bit, because something is better than nothing. And if you can't give to the beggar and the poor, at least offer some words of comfort, a greeting or a smile. What I am trying to say is that, you should show some compassion to another human being who is experiencing some really tough time, the same way you would like that others empathize with you if you were doing very bad.

The very words "In God we trust," printed on the dollar express clearly the fact that the majority of people in America are Christians. It is therefore paradoxical to see the majority of pedestrians ambulate in front of their fellow destitute human beings without paying them any mind, when it is obvious that many of them are Christians. Without trying to sound like a preacher, it is good for everybody to be reminded of the very teachings of the Christian bible concerning compassion for the poor.

It is written in the Christian Gospel that those who do not help the poor will not go to heaven, because by ignoring the poor homeless beggar, they are ignoring God himself. Sometimes people do not realize that Jesus himself -the savior of the world according to Christianity- was a homeless man who wandered from town to town and city to city without a place to call home. So, to worship Jesus a homeless man as your lord and savior, although you have never seen him, but at the same time find every excuse imaginable not to show compassion and not to help a homeless man or woman who is suffering right in front of your eyes, is contradictory.

This parable in the gospel of Matthew chapter 25: verses 31 to 46 is very emphatic about the anger of Jesus himself about the Christians who show no compassion for the homeless: *"When the Son of Man comes in his glory, and all the angels with him, he will sit on his glorious throne. All the nations will be gathered before him, and he will separate the people one from another as a shepherd separates the sheep from the goats. He will put the sheep on his right and the goats on his left. Then the King will say to those on his right, 'Come, you who are blessed by my Father; take your inheritance, the kingdom prepared for you since the creation of the world. For I was hungry and you gave me something to eat, I was thirsty and you gave me something to drink, I was a stranger and you invited me in, I needed clothes and you clothed me, I was sick and you looked after me, I was in prison and you came to visit me. Then the righteous will answer him, 'Lord, when did we see you hungry and feed you, or thirsty and give you something to drink? When did we see you a stranger and invite you in, or needing clothes and clothe you? When did we see you sick or in prison and go to visit you? The King will reply, 'Truly I tell you, whatever you did for one of the least of these brothers and sisters of mine, you did for me. Then he will say to those on his left, 'Depart from me, you who are cursed, into the eternal fire prepared for the devil and his angels. For I was hungry and you gave me nothing to eat, I was thirsty and you gave me nothing to drink, I was a stranger and you did not invite me in, I needed clothes and you did not clothe me, I was sick and in prison and you did not look after me. They also will answer, 'Lord,*

14

when did we see you hungry or thirsty or a stranger or needing clothes or sick or in prison, and did not help you? He will reply, 'Truly I tell you, whatever you did not do for one of the least of these, you did not do for me. Then they will go away to eternal punishment, but the righteous to eternal life."

RESPECT THE HOMELESS:

One time, this impeccably dressed rich looking white man walked to me with leftovers of a meal he had purchased in one of the fancy restaurants downtown. "This is a 40 dollar steak. I did not eat any of it. You can have it if you want", he said. "Yes, why not"? I responded. But before my stretched hand had a chance to grab the bag of food, he held it back and asked me this question, "What is your story?" "Long story," I answered. "I got time. I want to hear," He responded back. But truly speaking, I was reluctant to narrate my entire homeless misadventure, because it is too depressing and would take too much time. "Ok, it is either your story or that," he said while showing me the food. At that point, I really got offended and responded "Oh now you gonna blackmail me? "Fuck you then!" he said irately and walked away. "Fuck you too, you keep your food, I don't want it." I said back.

Because I am poor, homeless and in need, doesn't mean that I have to accept to be insulted, disrespected and humiliated for a piece of steak, no matter how much it costs. When you give to a beggar or a homeless, you have to understand that, he or she is a human being and deserves respect like anybody else. You have to give out of compassion, kindness and respect of their dignity.

Here is another anecdote: One day, a young white couple walked pass me and as soon as I said, "help the homeless," the man entered into a rage. "Don't talk to me nigger! Don't say nothing to me! Homeless bastard!"

he screamed back at me. I was speechless as I tried to rationalize the behavior of this man vomiting his hatred at me for no justifiable reasons, except that I was black and homeless and asked him for some change. He kept on cursing at me while walking away, and his girlfriend did not seem bothered at all. I was trying to figure out whether he was hating on me because I was black or homeless? Or both? Obviously both. I guess he was racist and homelessphobic. Wow, I have just created a neologism. So proud of myself. But all jokes aside, I want to say this to people who are unkind and mean to the homeless; yes, sometimes, we want to find all excuses in the book to justify our apathy, lack of compassion and resentment for the homeless: They are lazy, why don't they get a job? They are on drugs, they are crazy and so and so. What bothers me, is that many of those who react like that, go to church every Sunday and call themselves Christians. But such an attitude contradicts the very teachings of Christianity which can be summarized in the following verse in the Christian Holy book of the Bible, in the gospel of Luc Chapter 6 Verse 31: "*And just as you desire people to do for you, do for them*"(Aramaic Version Plain English).

So, my advice to everybody who is not homeless is this: Be grateful and consider it a blessing, that you have a roof over your head in a luxurious apartment, condo and house, and don't have to worry about sleeping on the streets, and go hungry like the homeless man and woman that you pass and scorn every day and night, when you go spend your hard earned money at fancy restaurants, bars, night clubs, sports and other entertainment venues.

Yes, you may be more fortunate than the homeless man or woman that you despise or fail to acknowledge as a human being like you, but you don't know what can happen to you that can be worse than his or her predicament. Think about this: You may go to a doctor's appointment the next day and be diagnosed with a terminal cancer. Wouldn't that be a worse predicament than that of the indigent who you shunned a night ago? Or you can cross the street after looking down on a homeless man or woman, get hit by a car and find yourself paralyzed for life and forced to use a wheelchair for the rest of your life. Then whose condition would be worse? You who have a roof over your head but can never recover from your disability for the rest of your life, or the homeless man or woman who can walk and come out of homelessness one day? And, a worst case scenario, you may go home after cursing, mistreating or disdaining a homeless person and never wake up in the morning after you go to sleep at night. So, consider yourself a blessed person for having a place to call home and the means to live a normal and stable life. And regardless of the causes of their tribulation, do not look down on or be apathetic towards those who are suffering and are forced to live like animals outside.

KICKING THE HOMELESS OUTSIDE IN THE COLD WINTER:

I had went to Union Station to use and fully charge my laptop so that, when I get to my tent and stay sheltered inside from the extreme cold outside, I could be able to play some chess game and listen to videos that I downloaded on my computer.

It was extremely cold outside indeed. I did not realize that it was past midnight when I got inside the station. But I had honestly thought that they would let the homeless stay inside Union Station during hypothermia weather because it is a health hazard for anybody to stay and sleep outdoors when it is below freezing outside.

But to my surprise, a security guard and his colleague walked up to an elderly homeless lady who looked old enough to be their grand-mother and ordered her to go outside or he would bar her permanently from the station. He then walked towards some other homeless men and women who were sitting in the main entrance lobby of the station and ordered them to leave. I took offense when he said to them, "This is not your house here." He told them that a van was waiting outside on the next block from the station to take them to an emergency shelter. There were other people in the station who obviously did not look homeless. When one of the white guys in the lobby asked him if the station was closing, he told them that he was not talking about them. All the homeless were black; so was the two security guards chasing them out. It was below zero degree outside and the snow on the sidewalk had turned into ice. I really doubted that there was really a van outside to take them to a warming center as he claimed. I had just came into the station and did not notice any van at the location that he indicated.

"They know this is not their house" I yelled at the security guard. "They don't act like they do" He responded. Obviously, he did not realize that I was homeless also, because he never said anything to me when he went around to ask anyone who seemed be homeless to exit the station. "You know that they don't have a place to go to and they are here because it is freezing outside; and you don't have to be mean to them by the way. They are human beings like you and you never know what can happen to you. You may lose your job one day and find yourself in a situation as bad as theirs. So stop being arrogant." I hollered back angrily. He was visibly annoyed by my reaction and walked away with the other security guard following behind him. I got up and headed outside to see if there was a van out there to take, to a warming center, the homeless who went outside. But there was no van on the corner of Massachusetts Avenue and North Capitol Street and nowhere in the vicinity; and those he chased out of the station were simply standing out in the icy cold. I went to the bus station across the street to catch a bus going in the direction of K and 16 streets, North West. One of the homeless who got kicked out of the station also, run to me from across North Capitol Street and asked me whether I had seen the hypothermia van. I told him that I did not. He was freezing and decided to walk to the next hypothermia emergency center which was at least 10 blocks away. At least he was able to walk a long distance through the icy cold. I worried about the elderly lady, who obviously would not think of walking that far through the life threatening weather to be sheltered. I was just devastated that a young black security guard could not have any compassion for a lady who was old enough to be his grandmother, but would simply throw her outside in the subzero winter weather. She could have frozen to death out there because nobody had made it their business to make sure that she got an emergency transportation to a shelter.

I waited in vain for my bus for a good hour. I guess the buses were not running on their regular schedule because of the winter storm. The hypothermia van did not show up either. I walked all the way to the 24 hour FedEx store on the 16th block of K Street, North West to do some work on my laptop and stay in a warm place until the morning.

FEED THEM WHAT YOU WILL EAT YOURSELF:

There are too many food kitchens and places in Washington DC where a homeless person can get a free meal and some free food. No homeless man or woman in this city should starve, unless he or she is lazy and refuses to make the effort to find a place where to go and get some free meal and food. It is therefore a blessing that the hungry, at least in this city, can count on compassionate and charitable individuals, groups, organizations and churches to feed, assist and help them.

There were times when I did not have a penny to afford a meal and did not have to worry either, because there was always somewhere where I could go to get free breakfast, lunch or dinner. Many of the places, mainly churches, take the time to prepare decent meals. On the other end, there are also certain of these organizations that really feed the homeless, food that they will not eat themselves. At times, I had forced myself to go to Salvation Army or Martha's Table food trucks to eat their food because I was very hungry and had no money. But, the food was very disgusting. I am not saying this to be ungrateful. The soup looked and tasted like they just grabbed anything they could find from the donated food cans, or gathered some old left-over food, and threw it in a big pot and cooked it.

Martha's Table's van, comes to feed the homeless at MacPherson Park every day between 5:30 to 6:00 pm. They always serve stale peanut butter sandwiches. You can barely tell the peanut butter from the jelly, because it has been glued together for so long. I doubt any of the volunteers on the van who distribute these sandwiches would ever eat one of them. The Salvation army's van, which also gives out dinner to the homeless every evening at various locations, from Union station at 6:00 pm to the corner of 14th Street and New York Avenue, North West, by 8:00pm, does also give out peanut butter sandwiches gone stale. But from time to time although very rarely, they give out decent soups and fresh peanut butter sandwiches. As soon as the Martha's Table and Salvation Army's vans leave, many, if not most of the peanut butter sandwiches end up on the benches or in the garbage cans not far from the feeding spot or are used by some of the homeless to feed the pigeons hanging around. My issue with these organizations is that, they are very popular and receive millions of dollars in funds from donors to feed the homeless. Therefore, they have the resources to at least, feed the homeless, fresh peanut butter sandwiches, instead of giving them sandwiches that were made and kept in fridges for a week or so.

.

NOT EASY FOR HOMELESS WOMEN:

I could have written a long litany of issues regarding the difficulties of homeless women, but I will cite these very few examples to show how harder it is for homeless women than homeless men out there.

I will start with a reality that I have seen at one of the largest homeless relief organization in Washington D.C. SOME -the acronym for (So Other People May Eat) - is a non-profit organization that provides services to the homeless and runs the most frequented soup kitchen in Washington DC. They open every day of the year and serve breakfast and lunch. Many U.S Presidents, like George Bush and Bill Clinton, had visited that place and served meals to the homeless during their visits there. The staff at SOME are supposed to provide services to homeless men and women equally, but the truth is that they treat homeless women as second class citizens, while homeless men are treated better.

I do not understand why the homeless women have to wait outside in the cold from 7:00 am until 8:30 am to eat breakfast, and then still wait outside again, until 10:00 am before they can take a shower. Every morning, the homeless men and women start lining up outside for breakfast by 6:00am, no matter how hot or cold it is. The staff opens the doors at precisely 7:00 am for everybody to enter and go directly inside the dining room, and wait for meals to be served at 7:20 am. When the dining room fills up, those who are waiting for it to be emptied, cleaned and opened again at 8:00 am, can, if they are male, wait inside the building's waiting room where it is warm and heated or cooled with fans and air-conditioners, depending on the seasons of the year. But even if it is freezing cold and below zero degree temperature during the winter, or sizzling hot in the summer, the homeless women are asked to wait outside. The reason is that, women are not allowed in the waiting room when men are taking their shower and vice versa. Truth of the matter is that, it is not possible for someone in the waiting room to see anybody, male or female, who is in the showers and showers area. So, it should not be a problem for homeless women to wait inside the waiting room as their male counterparts until the dining room opens back up for breakfast. And really, the issue could easily be solved by putting, either a door or a curtain at the entrance of the bathroom. Also, SOME has enough funds to build extra showers by expanding some of the buildings on the property. The homeless women who need to go to work early in the morning like the homeless men, must be able to take a shower as early as the men and not wait until 10:00 am.

Even the clothing room used to have women wait until 10:00 am to get clothes, while men were served first, from 9:00 am to 10:00 am for years until very recently. Now, men and women get their clothes at the same time from 8:00 am to 9:00 am.

SOME is by no means an exception when it comes to the ill-treatment of homeless women. I find it unbelievable that a place like Bethany, also known as N Street Village, which is a day shelter for homeless women, requires them do a chore in order to receive services there (which include   mail, breakfast, lunch, shower, laundry or simply stay there until they close in the afternoon for the day). There was another homeless women day center called Rachel -which used to be on 11st NW; but is now closed- where homeless women were also asked to do a chore as a condition to receive services. But, I have never heard of, or been to any day shelter for homeless men, where men were asked to perform some chores in order to get services.

It is evident that there are more homeless men than homeless women on the street. But it is disheartening to see so many homeless women sleeping outside because when they go to the shelters for homeless women, they are told that there is no more beds available. I can understand that a woman sleeps outside because she refuses to go to a shelter for whatever reason. But I do not understand why there are not enough shelters for women.

I am a man, yet I find it very hard to be a homeless on the street. I can't imagine what it is like for a woman to be homeless. But I can see how hard it is for them to survive out there and how terrible they are treated, even by those who claim to be helping the homeless. It is very dangerous for homeless women to sleep outside because they are exposed to male predators and rapists. I have heard so many homeless women tell me that they were attacked, beaten and raped while sleeping at night outside.

THE SOCIAL WORKER WHO WAS MEAN TO ME:

Many homeless are reluctant to go to places where they can get services because the social workers there do not treat them with respect, sometimes.

Here is a personal experience. It was located in a house on 11th street N.W, not far from the Washington D.C downtown area, but it is closed now because of the gentrification which is occurring in Washington D.C. Newly-built luxurious condos and apartments are changing the demographic of most areas of the city. Poor and low-income people are forced to move out and wealthier white middle class people move in. Although it was primarily a day shelter for women, Rachel had also a program for men in the basement of the building, accessible through the back alley. Homeless men could take showers, receive mails and get their clothes washed there three days a week when they opened for four hours regularly.

I used the place as my primary mailing address for over 10 years, although I had not gone there frequently for the last couple of years. I started going back there to take a shower, whenever I could not make it on time to SOME where I had been taking showers regularly. I never had any problem with the friendly social workers who used to work there in the past. But, the new social worker there was bizarre and unfriendly to me since the first day I met him. Although that day, I politely greeted him, introduced myself and informed him that I used to come there regularly in the past.

I told him that I wanted to take a shower. He told me to sign the shower list and wait. I did. He went back playing cards with some of the homeless guys and put on a movie.

It did not seem right to watch a salaried social worker spend his time watching movies, playing cards and entertaining himself, in the company of homeless men who had no job and should not be encouraged to waste their time idling; and surely not in the company of those who were supposed to help them get back on their feet. Obviously, many of the homeless guys were coming there not to get help or services. They came there only to kill time and wait for a meal while being entertained, as they lingered around until it was time for the place to close for the day. A couple of times, I watched him doze off and snore at his desk, after he had played cards and eaten the very meal he had served to the homeless men there.

I used to go there, wait until it was time to take my shower and left right after, because I did not like the vibes there. Normally, when the meal was ready, he called and served everybody in the kitchen, at the back of the place, and saved a plate for whoever was in the shower. But one time, he started serving meal when I was in the shower, but when I came out of the shower and asked him if I could get a plate -thinking that he had set a plat aside for me-, he got enraged and said to me that, before I went to the bathroom, I should have told him that I wanted to eat so that he would have saved me a plate. I was surprised because I have seen

28

him setting a plate aside for whoever was in the shower without that person asking him to. I just did not respond because obviously he did not want to serve me for whatever reason and was simply finding excuses to blame and frustrate me. He told me to hold on as if he was about to go to the kitchen to serve me, but instead he kept on playing cards for at least 10 minutes until I simply got up in desperation. But before I proceeded to the door to leave, he told the guys to hold on and went to the kitchen and brought me a plate.

One time, I needed a shower desperately after I had stayed in my tent and not showered for two straight days, because of uninterrupted freezing slushy rains falling without interruption for almost two days. When the weather became clement, I rushed to the center but there was a note on the door saying that the place was closed for that day. In the note, the social worker mentioned that he had an emergency, but would re-open the center for service the next day at the same hours (4:00pm to 6:30pm).

I returned the next day at 4:10 pm and knocked on the door. The social worker opened it and told me that nobody else showed up, therefore he was closing the place. I told him that it was only 10 minutes past 4:00 pm and I needed a shower very bad, because I had not taken any in three days. He insisted that he had something else to do and that I had to come back the morning of the next day when the center opens on its regular schedule. I persisted in vain that I needed a shower badly but he repeated that I should come back the next day. The real issue was that the man was simply lazy and did not want to clean the shower after me. He figured out that it was very unlikely that anybody else would show up and used that as an excuse to close the place early and not worry about doing any work. He told me that the guy who helps him clean the bathroom did not show up, so there were nobody to clean the bathroom after me. I did not understand because he was the one getting paid to do the job. He did not change his mind and instead closed the door, while I stood there totally confused. He had gotten accustomed to laze around and have another homeless man, clean the bathroom and sweep and mop the place, and basically do his work, after playing cards and idling around in his company, all day.

I decided to walk around to the front of the building and go upstairs to talk to whoever was in charge of the center. But they had already left because the office had closed at 4:00pm as usual.

I walked down the street and explained what happened to a homeless lady acquaintance who used to go to the woman program. She suggested that I call Rachel's office and leave a message for the boss lady there. I did. The next morning, a lady named Michelle, who identified herself as the director of both women and men programs at Rachel, returned my call and told me that she received my message. She acknowledged that I was right, because I showed up on time and even if nobody else showed up, I was there and was supposed to receive service accordingly. She apologized to me, assured me that it will never happen again and told me that I could come and take a shower there at any time that I desired according to the program's schedule.

I thanked and told her that I would come the next day, which I did. As soon as I showed up there, the social worker in question got very enraged. He told me that he was the one in charge of the program downstairs, and that I had no business going to report what happened there to the lady upstairs. I told him that the lady Michelle, had told me that she was the director of both men and women's programs. He just stared at me and could not utter a word because he was so irritated. "Go ahead, I will let you take a shower today!" he mumbled after catching his breath.

He instructed his homeless flunky, who does all the work for him, to hand me a towel and insisted that I take my shower and leave. It was a way to let me know that I was not welcomed to wait for the meal to be ready, although I normally do not anyway. "What you mean, you will let me take a shower today?" "Are you saying that I can't come here to take a shower here anymore?" I answered back to him. Obviously he could not give me a straight answer. I went and took my shower as fast as I could and left, because I was totally turned off by the negative atmosphere. I returned there a week or two later and thought that the center had already opened, but actually I had showed up eight minutes sooner without realizing it. I knocked on the door. He opened it, saw me, and shut it back without saying a word to me.

I immediately assumed that he was denying me access to the center. I walked back to the front of the building and rang the bell of the main office. But he showed up to the door, upstairs. "How can I help you?" he said sarcastically, with a smirk on his face. "I want to talk to the director" I responded coolly. "Yeah! Let me go get her because we got to solve this problem" he added. Few seconds later, he showed up with the lady, his boss. I told her that I was the homeless person who had called her to complain about him for not letting me take a shower the last time. I told her that I had no problem with him and did not understand why he was being nasty to me. I explained that I had knocked on the door and he simply slammed it back to my face without saying anything to me. She explained to me that I had come few minutes sooner and that it was just time for the center to open. I told her that I did not know that I had got there few minutes earlier, and that he did not say anything to me but just shut the door in my face. He denied it and claimed that he had told me that he was on the phone and that the center would open in few minutes. He was lying and the lady seemed not to believe him anyway. She just repeated to me to go downstairs, take my shower and not to worry. When I went downstairs, he told me in a very mean manner to take my shower and leave. You can run back upstairs and tell her" he added. "Why are you messing with me?" I said to him. "I mess with you because I feel like it" He responded. "Look, I am not going to pay you any mind" I retorted. I went in the shower to wash and left out right after, and never returned there ever.

Since then, I tried to get up early in the morning and go to SOME to be able to take a shower between 7:00 am to 9:00 am. When I could not make it on time at SOME, I simply walked for 10 minutes to the corner store down the street to buy a one gallon bottle of water, and go back to my tent and take a cold shower outside.

I became used to buying some one-gallon water bottles and take a cold shower outside of my tent, when I could not make it on time to SOME where I used to take my shower after the incident at Rachel. But, to be able to take a shower there, you have to show up and sign the shower list by 7:30 am to be lucky enough to be among the 40 people allowed on that list. One morning I got there too late to make it on the shower list. I was so frustrated because I needed a shower very bad. I saw a friend of mine coming to get breakfast there and I asked him whether he knew another place where I could take shower. "St Aloysius," He told me. I used to go there long time ago but I forgot that the place was still open for business. I run up there. It was about 8 o'clock. I signed the shower list there and took a very nice shower. I have been going there since, because the folks working there are very nice and friendly and make it easy for a homeless man to get services there. Reggie, the gentleman who does the showers and laundry, is an extremely nice and friendly guy. Even when I get there late and can't make it to the list, he always makes an effort to get me to take a shower and simply reminds me to try to make it sooner next time.

CHAPTER 2

WHY ARE YOU HOMELESS?

I saw puzzlement and dejection in the faces of some of the folks who have seen me begging on the street corner. "Why are you homeless" is surely the question they desired to ask me. Quite often, they did put the question to me directly. Normally, I decline to answer because when I think about it, it upsets me.

One day, I was approached by a clean cut white gentleman dressed in a dark suit and a red tie. He probably had left the bar next door. He was noticeably inebriated. The conversation revolved around me, my homeless story, politics and life in general. He could not understand why a person like me who seemed intelligent was homeless. I went on and told him my story. He left after we had a chat for half an hour. A week later, I saw him again. He was sober this time but his demeanor was inimical. He spoke to me menacingly by asking me what he should do, if he sees me again at the same spot in two weeks. I was at awe and had a hard time understanding what he was getting at. But I kept my cool and told him that I was working on improving my condition, and that hopefully things will get better in a near future. He acted like he did not understand why I was homeless and as if I was simply lazy and did not try to make things better for myself, although I took the time to explain everything to him in detail. He walked away with a very mean look on his face. Two weeks later, I saw him again. He sat on the wall by a window of the building where I was sitting as usual. He started again with his threats as if to suggest that if he sees me again in the next few weeks, I would face some unpleasant consequences, without being specific. Although, I calmly tried again to assure him that I was making some effort to come out of my predicament, he yelled back "You always repeat the same story". At that point, I got offended. I said to him "I did not have to tell you anything about me to start with. But I did because you sat here and asked me why I was homeless and I thought you really cared to know. So, that is your problem if you don't believe anything I said". I then calmed down, pulled out my laptop and told him that I had been working on some project that I could not finish because my laptop had broken down and I needed to take it to the store to be fixed. "Why didn't you take it to the store then?" he retorted. "Because I just didn't yet, but I will, tomorrow or the following day, as soon I can make enough money for transportation, since it costs me at least $12 to travel back and forth, on the subway train, to the store in Fairfax Virginia where I purchased the computer." I responded. Then I continued: "You see me panhandling here; this is how I raised enough money to buy this laptop for $499 at Micro Center in Fairfax, Virginia". "I paid a $100 for a one- year warranty on it, so there will fix it for free," I said to him. "No, they won't fix it," he responded and asked me to hand him the computer so he will see it. "I just told you I got a warranty for hardware damage on the computer. So, why won't they fix it?" I asked him. "Because it is a stolen property," he replied. I got infuriated by his answer. "Oh, you assume that because I am a homeless and a black person begging on the street, I must have stolen this laptop? "So I spent all this time trying to explain to you that, the money I make by begging on the street is what I have saved and used to purchase this computer and do other things to improve my situation, but you thought I was just lying? "So you really think I am a thief? "You are really insulting me," I told him. But he persisted by asking me to hand him the computer. He gave me the impression that he was some kind of law enforcement agent who wanted to get hold of the computer to confiscate it as a stolen property. He even told me that I was being recorded while holding and leaning toward the collar of his costume. I was aggravated and speechless at that point and let him know that I had nothing else to say to him. I kept ignoring him as he kept pressing me to hand him the computer. He left after making more threats about seeing me again in a week. Few weeks later I saw him again. "You mad at me?" He said. "You disrespected me by calling me a thief, and telling me that I stole my own laptop, although I told you that I bought it." I responded. "Can I sit and talk to you?" he said. I was reluctant but he did sit next to me anyway. At that point I put out the laptop. I had already taken to the store and had it repaired by then. "You told me that they would not fix it because it was stolen property, right?" I said to him as I turned it on. "Let me see it" He said again. "Nope"! I don't trust you," I said. "I still believe you stole it," He countered. I kept my cool, turned the laptop's camera on and rotated it towards him. "Oh you really believe I stole this laptop because I am a black homeless man, although I told you that I purchased it and in which store and where? "I am putting this on YouTube." I said while holding the laptop with the camera focused on his face. He turned his face away and said "no, no, no"; then got up and walked away. I have not seen him until long after and he never bothered me since.

Most of the time, I am reluctant to tell my story when someone asks me why am I homeless, because people doubt whatever you tell them that does not fit into the stereotypes they have of a homeless person.

Most people assume that homeless are alcoholics or drug addicts. Although it is undeniable that a great number of homeless are suffering from alcohol and drug addiction, there are also a lot of homeless who are not homeless because of alcohol or drug addiction and do not have any substance abuse issue.

Here is an example. I was at McPherson Park in North West Washington D.C, not far from the White house one Sunday afternoon. A young lady, who was among a group of young protesters rallying in DC against the IMF and the World Bank, approached me and said: "Wow look how red your eyes are; you got that good weed. Where that good weed at?" There were also few other times when young protesters from out of town approached me and asked if I could help them get some marijuana. I wear dread locks for ideological reasons and not because I smoke marijuana. So if I tell a person that I do not smoke marijuana, they still will not believe it because they do not understand that my eyes are red because I sleep outside and am not getting adequate sleep.   But in actuality, I do not drink alcohol; I do not smoke anything including cigarettes and I definitely do not consume any narcotic. I am too afraid to put in me anything that will have a controlling effect on me.

Most people assume that the homeless are crazy people. Well, I will not deny that a lot of homeless people suffer from mentally illnesses. It is obvious in the abnormal and asocial behavior that many homeless exhibit on the streets. Years ago, government run mental institutions all over the country included St Elizabeth hospital in Washington DC, had released a large number of mentally ill individuals on the streets. This is why you see so many mentally ill homeless out there. It is also evident that harsh and degrading conditions can mentally affect anyone subjected to homelessness.

I will be in denial if I claim that homelessness has not affected me emotionally, psychologically and mentally in any shape, way or form. Off course, I get frustrated, depressed, upset and act unbecomingly sometimes like any other normal person. But, I do not talk to myself or to invisible beings. No, I do not eat out of trash cans. No, I do not blame the government or the world for everything that is wrong with me. No, I do not urinate or defecate on myself. Whatever crazy, unproductive, excessive or out of control behavior I may exude for whatever reasons, I am still conscious of my actions and wrongdoings. So, I consider myself normal although only a psychiatrist can confirm that with certitude.

One day, I got very stressed-out about my homeless predicament after I had just left the Randall Shelter in South West, Washington DC. It was one of the few shelters where I ever stayed some years ago, when I became homeless for the first time. I was so worried that my mental health could be affected by homelessness. I closed my eyes and made the following prayer "God, take everything from me, but please do not touch my mind".

Since I have been homeless, I have made of my mental health a prime concern. I have always been very careful, not to allow myself to stay depressed or too frustrated to the point of desperation. I even had the obsession of studying mental illnesses and their symptoms, so that I will stay alert and seek help immediately in case I noticed warning signs indicating that I may have crossed the line and erred into abnormality in my behavior.

Now, the stereotype that people are homeless because they are lazy and do not want to work does not apply to me. As I explained in the next chapter, I love to work. So, I am not the stereotypical homeless.

Now, the reason why I am homeless is unimportant and beside the point because I did not cause it to happen to me. I am just a victim of misfortune. That is the best way I can put it. Everything terrible that happens to a person is not necessarily self-inflicted. You cannot just conclude that a person made the choice to be homeless. I did not choose to be homeless. I just had a bad luck. I hear some people say that there is no such a thing as bad luck. So if you find yourself on a street corner and someone runs up to you with a weapon and rob you, isn't that bad luck? To me it is, because you were at the wrong place at the wrong time. If the train you are on, derails and you get injured, to me it is bad luck because you are a victim of an accident that you did not cause. If you get food poisoned after dining at a reputable restaurant, to me that is bad luck because you did not plan to get sick when you went to dine out with friends and relatives.

So, whether I became homeless by my own fault or for reasons beyond my control, I understand that it is still my responsibility to solve the crisis I find myself in. There is therefore no excuse for us to simply expect a problem we face to solve itself.

My homeless journey has taught the misfortunate sufferer that I am, that trials and tribulations can be either constructive or destructive. Although I cannot control my fate, I can nonetheless, deal with the way it affects me and the way I respond to and navigate through it. My mind is mine. I can choose to either allow circumstances to stress me and make things worse, or be mentally strong in the face of adversity and make things better. Homelessness taught me, that in coping with agony, hardship and fatality, I can either be weak enough to incarcerate my soul into powerlessness and gloom or strong enough to liberate my mind from hopelessness and doom.

CHAPTER 3:

WHY DON'T YOU GO TO A SHELTER?

Some of the good people, who have seen me outside in the freezing cold and asked me whether I would go to a homeless shelter to stay out of the cold, seemed shocked when I responded that I would not.

To be honest, I have nothing against homeless shelters. I think they are needed and very helpful to thousands of homeless men and women, who are able to have a temporary roof over their head in a warm place for at least a night. Actually, I used to go to homeless shelters, when I became homeless the first time around. At first, I was spending the nights trying to sleep on park benches but I would doze off and wake up, off and on, during the whole night, because I was worried about anybody approaching me in my sleep, and messing with me. One night, I did not feel like sleeping on benches; so I ambled around for hours, until I walked into a street light pole and felt an excruciating pain in my forehead, because I was literally sleep-walking with my eyes closed. I screamed and held my forehead. "Enough of this! I am going to a shelter," I told myself. This is how I started going to homeless shelters. But, until I was able to make enough money and afford to move to a cheap room in a rooming house a year or two later, I had to force myself to go shelters.

The first problem with most homeless shelters in Washington DC is that they are overnight shelters, which means that the homeless can only go in after 6:00 pm and must leave by 6:00 am, with all their possessions. Every night, you are assigned a different bed on a first come first served basis. If the person who slept the night before on the bed that you are assigned to, have bed bugs or fleas on his body or in his garments, you will most likely be at risk of catching them. I had got infected with fleas and bed bugs in shelters so many times.

I used to stash my belongings in bushes somewhere not too far from the shelter. They were exposed to the rain and to other homeless who would not hesitate to steal another homeless person's belongings. I dealt with some of the inconveniences of going to shelters because I clearly understood that a shelter is not a hotel but just a place to spend the night indoors instead of outside.

Here are the real problems about the shelters that made me unwilling to go into any of them this time. To me, it was like torturing myself to be in a dorm or a trailer with few other homeless men who obviously did not shower for god-knows-how-long, and wore the same stinky and filthy clothes for ever after consuming alcohol all day and pissing on themselves. Can you imagine the odor that comes out of a mixture of alcohol, body sweat, urine and dirty clothes? Sometimes, I was in my bunk and when the homeless man next to me took his shoes off, I was forced to smell his stinking feet all night. I used to wake up with migraines in the morning after trying very hard to ignore the stench and sleep through it.

Another problem I had with shelters is that, I could not sleep when I was unfortunate enough to have a schizophrenic in a bunk or bed next to me, who talked out loud to a wall or to some invisible being while sitting on his bed, in the dark, all night. And again, I don't know if that was worse than a fat dude who snored so loud. I snore too, but I just can't sleep in a dorm with four or five guys snoring out loud and a couple of crazy dudes speaking to themselves loudly all night. After I moved out into a rooming house from the last shelter I was in, I could no longer imagine myself ever going to a homeless shelter and subject myself to such agony, even for the comfort of a warm bed in the winter.

THE GUYS TRYING TO SET ME ON FIRE:

I did not realize how dangerous it was to live on the street, until some young men tried to burn me while I was sleeping in a back alley. It happened a Saturday night around 9 o'clock after I had come back to the alley where I used to sleep every night, grabbed some cardboards that I normally stashed around, used them to build a little shelter inside a loading dock and garage space, and went to sleep.

Every night, I and few other homeless guys and a homeless couple, slept there after the workers who parked their cars there, had left. I smelled some smoke while I was dozing off. I rushed outside the cardboard structure and saw part of it catching fire and put the fire out. None of the other homeless had come back yet. When they did, I told them that somebody had set my card board structure on fire while I was sleeping, but I was lucky enough to smell the smoke and get up in time to put it off. One of the homeless guys told me that one time, while he was sleeping, someone threw a hard metal object at him, but when he woke up he did not see anybody. He was fortunate enough because he did not get injured. I wondered who could be so evil to come and try to harm poor homeless folks in their sleep. But I finally got the answer to my question few Saturday nights later. The homeless couple who slept in the same garage had covered with blankets, the steps under which they slept, as they usually did every night, so that they could keep warm and have some privacy. Nobody else was there.

46

I walked into the alley from the H street side and went to grab my cardboards to build my little shelter and go to sleep. When I was approaching the garage, I saw about three white teenagers creeping inside the garage by the blanket-covered -stairs and about to set the blankets on fire. The homeless couple sleeping inside had no idea what was going on outside. I walked back to the dumpster behind which I kept my cardboards, and grabbed a metal pole that I had stashed there, in expectation of having to face one day, whoever were coming to try to harm us. Before they had the time to set the blankets on fire, they saw me walking to them with the pole and ready to hit them. They run towards the exit of the alley on the 13th street side. I chased behind them and saw them get into a car parked outside the alley and drive away. These juveniles had nothing better to do but spend their weekend night going to alleys to try to burn and use heavy objects to harm sleeping homeless people.

MY TENT IN THE WOODS:

I took a bike ride northbound on North capital Avenue. It separates the east and west parts of the city of Washington D.C, from the Northern side of the U.S Capitol building to the border with the city of Silver Spring in the state of Maryland. When I reached the overpass above Irving Street, I saw in front of me the ideal site; I mean, a picturesque grassy and wooded open space with a lot of bushes and trees in the surroundings. I chose a tree where I set up camp. The area was very peaceful. The human activities around there were limited to sporadic movements of very few pedestrians on Irving Street and scarcely any on North Capitol Street, mostly in the daytime and rarely at night. There is also the commuter traffic on North Capitol Street and its connecting and exit roads; and also on Irving Street, which runs underneath and perpendicular to North Capitol Street.

Also, as far as visible buildings, from the little hill where my tent is located, towards the south, I can see the fenced back of the Washington Veteran Administration Hospital which is located on the grounds of the Washington Hospital center, across Irving Street. Towards the north, across a road connecting Irving and North Capitol streets, I can see the fence edged by bushes, of an estate which is the property of US army, and where the Armed Forces Retirement Home and The old Soldiers Golf Course are located. Towards the east, there is a panoramic view of the Basilica of the National Shrine of the Immaculate Conception, which elevates majestically atop of the flora, with its blue dome glowing in the dark night. Towards the West, Irving Street vanishes in the scenery of fences, bushes, shrubs and trees outside of the U.S army property on the right side, and barely visible buildings inside the fenced Washington Hospital center on the left side.

It was the fall season and I did not need too much to get settled. I came back the next day with a backpack with a blanket, a bedsheet and a tarp stuffed in it. I roamed in back alleys of houses half-a-mile down the street and came across a trashed but passably clean mattress. I dragged it all the way to my spot in the middle of the night because I did not want anybody to see me. I covered the mattress with the bedsheet and myself with the blanket and slept out there in the wild. The next day, I roamed again in some back alleys and found a larger blue dusty 20-foot-wide- by-30-foot-long tarp in a back of a construction site. The following day, I stopped at a CVS store and bought a rope. I knotted one end of the rope around the center of a stick and tossed it to a big branch above me and luckily it hooked at the intersection of a branch and a shoot. I pulled hard on it to make sure it would hold during a storm, but it did not budge. I grabbed the larger tarp and folded it diagonally, then held the rope tight and tied the top of the folded tarp. Then I moved the mattress underneath the tarp, and stretched the tarp around it. Then, I used a knife to cut pieces of dead branches and shaped one of the edges of each of them in a nail form, then used them to nail the tarp to the ground around the mattress. I ended up creating a tent in a rounded triangle shape like native-Americans' teepees. Then, I laid the smaller tarp on the ground and laid the mattress on it so that when it rains, the bottom of the mattress won't get soaked.

Two months later, about a week before thanksgiving of 2013, I heard a car horn blow while I was fixing to go to sleep. When I peeped out, I saw an SUV parked outside on the Road about ninety feet away. A man walked out and made a few steps in my direction. I got a bit frightened because it was dark at night, and I could not see his face or the object he was holding, which could have been a gun. But he was also prudent since he stopped at a distance and shouted "Hey my friend, I have a present for you, would you accept it if I bring it to you?" I felt at ease at that point and comforted that, he was not there to cause me harm, but instead, to express his kindheartedness to a homeless man sleeping underneath a tree by a highway. "Yes off course" I responded.

He proceeded to walk towards me with a cardboard box in his hand and said while handing it to me "I bought you a tent. You can use the tarp as a canopy above it". I was very happy. I thanked and told him that I was very grateful. He also asked me whether I needed a sleeping bag. I could not refuse. He promised to bring it by the following week, and he did. I assembled the tent the afternoon of the following day before it turned dark. It was a very –easy-to-assemble, nine foot long, seven foot wide and forty six Inch tall, blue, yellow and white, Northwest Territory tent. I looked around construction sites' dumpsters and found a large plastic sheet. I placed it underneath the tent to mitigate any penetration of rainwater inside from the ground, in case of heavy rains, since I had laid the tent straight on the ground. I never saw the man who brought me the tent again since the last time he came back to bring me the sleeping bag. But I will always be grateful to him because he was and will always be an angel as far as I am concerned. I know he will and probably did receive abundance of blessings in his life for being so carrying and generous. I am so thankful because I am still sleeping in that tent two years later. It had helped me throughout all seasons of the year also, and no rain or snow could get inside it, even during snow storms. While I was checking in back alleys to scavenge anything I could use, I found a small therapeutic mattress, inserted it into the tent and superposed it to the other larger but flatter mattress that I already had. I had enough space in the area between the tarp and the tent to keep my clothes and belongings inside.

Besides the guy who offered me the tent, very few other people stopped by occasionally, to bring me some food, water and blankets. When I had first got to the spot, there was a white man who used to come by every Saturday morning and bring me some canned food, juice and water. The last time he brought me some food, he told me that he was going to be gone out of town. I have not seen him since. Also, few days before my first thanksgiving in the tent, an Asian lady who spoke English with a perfect American accent brought me a blanket and gave me a 20 dollar bill. On Thanksgiving

Day she came back again to bring me a thanksgiving dinner. Few weeks later, on Christmas, I had left early in the morning to go to the downtown area, but when I returned at night, I found, by my tent, a dinner box in a plastic bag, and an envelope with a merry Christmas card with a $20 bill inside. A week later, on New Year day, a middle-eastern or Spanish-looking guy brought me some sandwiches and cans of soda. Last but not the least, in the beginning of this past summer, a guy with deadlocks and a Jamaican accent, brought me some clothes and a heavy bucket full of rusty coins; most of them pennies. I bought some vinegar and salt and cleaned them, then took them to a Safeway store and dumped them in their Coinstar coin machine. I made two trips because I did not clean all the coins the same day. I made about $40 in total from all the pennies. On very rare occasions, very few other people came by and dropped some bottles of water.

At least, at my new spot, nobody has ever bothered me although there are cars riding by and pedestrians occasionally walking down the road. I always find my belongings intact and untouched, when I return to my tent every night and day. At least I do not have to worry about other homeless guys or anybody stealing my possessions when I am away. The only occasional intruders are some field mice which invite themselves inside the tent, in my absence. Sometimes, they sneak in and munch on the bottom of the mattress while I am inside and sleeping. I normally make sure that I do not let any food and crumbs inside the tent. On two or three rare occasions, I came across one field mouse inside my tent when I got there, but as soon as it sensed my presence, it run out of the tent and disappeared in the grass. I normally make the effort not to kill any mouse that I catch in my tent. I simply chase them out of there. They have dug holes all around the tree by the tent. In order to make it hard for the mice to simply creep in and out of the tent, I covered the ground underneath it with a hard sheet of plastic and pulled its edges tight to at least 3 feet upward, all around and against the tent.

I keep a cooler around and store all exposed food in it to make sure more dangerous predators would not be attracted by left-overs. I assume that there is no bears or wolves in the area, but there is always a possibility of wild animals, roaming in an area where there is a verdant vegetation with almost no human presence. I have tucked a butcher knife and a four foot long metal bar under my mattress for protection, in case I faced danger and threat to my life from dangerous animals and human beings. I will admit that I am less worried about wild animals than humans, for the simple fact that animals would harm you only when they see you as a threat to their life, or when you look like food to them. But Humans will simply harm you for no justifiable reasons like the case of the kids who tried to set me and other homeless people on fire, for the fun of it.

The night of May 6, 2015, I was in my tent, listening to the news on my little radio about the horrific murder of a wealthy man, his wife, his son and their housekeeper. The intruders in the six-million-dollar mansion-which is located few blocks from the residency of the Vice-

President of the United States-therefore in a very affluent and secure neighborhood- kidnapped and brutally killed their victims after getting away with a forty thousand dollar ransom.

I immediately thought about this. Here I am, sleeping every night in a tent with no door in the wilderness where it gets dark at night despite the presence of few streetlights on the roads nearby and anybody with an evil intention can come and harm me while I am deep asleep, and nobody may see what happened. The irony is that, when I was staying in an apartment off West Virginia Avenue in Northeast Washington DC where I was renting a room, I would get up two or three times at night, and go check the front door and the windows to make sure they were locked. But I go to sleep in a tent under a tree every night out in the open and am not experiencing the same fear and worry, as when I was in an apartment with secured doors and windows. I know it is insane and crazy. I would not deny that I did entertain the thought that there could be wild animals like bears, wolves, and even raccoons who could pay me unexpected visits. But after spending several nights and months there, it was obvious that besides dears, a fox that I saw one night, a coyote that also came within distance another night because of the scent of a warm plate of fish I was about to eat outside my tent, one or two squirrels, and a stray cat which approached my tent occasionally, there were no dangerous animals in the area. I seriously considered adopting the cat, but my health condition did not allow me to. I was born with severe asthma and had a miserable childhood because of asthma attacks. I was fortunate enough when my asthma disappeared when I was about 16 year old. But, I am extremely allergic to cat hair. When I am exposed to it, I develop instantly an asthma-like attack. My chest gets so heavy and I can barely breathe. It is so painful to not be able to breathe. But I have not seen that cat since last year. I don't know what happened to it. Hopefully it found its way to an environment where humans could adopt it instead of living in the wild.

There is a squirrel that was living in the tree above my tent and did not come close to me at first even when I decided to feed it. I have fed squirrels before in the park by the convention center. They are used to human beings, and will come and get food out of your hand, although they would not let you fondle them. With time, my new squirrel buddy started coming closer and closer, until it got used to me. It got used to showing up in front of my tent every morning around 6:30 to 7:00 am, at exactly around the time that I had to get up to leave for the day. When I do not see it, I call out Squi, Squi, Squi, which is the name I gave it, and when it hears my calls, it runs to me, and snatches the food when I stretch my hand out of the tent. But when I am standing up, it only comes no closer than ten feet. Unfortunately, I have not seen Squi since the summer and it is winter now. Curiously, I have only seen one new squirrel around, but it does not come close enough to me, and I had the opportunity to feed it only a couple of times, and from a distance.

THE DEAD DEAR BY MY TENT:

I had just got to my spot late at night and noticed an animal lying next to a tree at about fifty feet from my tent. A first, because of my poor vision, I could not tell what it was, or whether it was dead or alive. Could it be a wolf which was wounded or just resting? I wondered anxiously. I grabbed a stick and prudently tiptoed toward the animal, until I could clearly see that it was a dead dear. I went back to my tent, got a couple of sheets of paper towel , grabbed one leg of the dear and dragged it close to the road, so that drivers could see it in the morning and call the authorities to remove it. But, to my surprise, when I returned from downtown later that night, the dead animal was still at the same spot. I went to sleep while the carcass was still lingering around. At least, I was relieved that the ground was covered with snow and the weather was icy cold, which meant that the dear's corpse would not rot and attract vultures.

When I woke up in the morning, I waited until around 10:00 am and called the city's animal removal service. A lady answered and told me that, she had already received a couple of calls, and that a team was on their way to remove the dear. I left after that.

The dead dear was still there for the third night, when I returned that night. I decided to drag it very close to the road surface, so that the drivers would see it right in their face as soon as they slow down at the intersection, when they were about to turn into the highway. I don't know, whether the city did come to remove it or someone picked it up and put it in his trunk to go use it as food, but, that dead dear was gone when I came back to my tent the fourth night.

EVICTION NOTICE:

One night, while I was returning from the city's downtown area, I noticed a metal sign post about 20 feet from my tent. It was dark but I approached it and read it. These words were written on it:

"NOTICE

The District of Columbia will conduct a general clean-up of this area

ON AND AFTER

After the date above this area will be designated as clean and may be cleaned again without additional notice. All personal belongings visible from this location, not removed from this public space by the date, and time listed above, shall be cleaned and disposed of at any time after the above stated cleanup time. Personal belongings, in plain sight, considered to be of obvious value (i.e., significant personal documents such as ID's, driver's licenses, passports, photographs, financial records, and other similar documents), will be temporary placed in storage and can be claimed in person within 30 days, by contacting THE Department of Human Services at 202-698-4170.

FURTHER INFORMATION AND ASSISTANCE CAN BE OBTAINED FROM:

The Department of Human Services 202-698-4170

The Community Partnership at 202-543-5298 ext. 101

The Washington Legal Clinic for the Homeless at 202-328-5000".

Although the sign talked about trash, the underlying message was that I had to move my tent and all belongings by the date on the notice, otherwise the city Department of public works would remove my belongings, which would be considered trash.

I knew that this was coming because a month earlier, on a very hot day, a white man and a black lady who worked for the city's homeless outreach service, came by to hand me some water and advise me to go to a shelter. The man said to me that the mayor (Vincent Gray, then) did not want any homeless to sleep outside and that, where I was located was too close to the streets, therefore too dangerous. I told him that I had been staying at the same location since the previous summer and stayed there throughout the winter, and never felt in harm way. But I knew that his words were some kind of threats and warnings about future actions to get me out of there. I also had that feeling when one day, I saw a white man walking his dog not far from my tent, although there is no residences in the immediate surroundings. So why would anybody who did not live anywhere around, would come to walk his dog so close to a homeless man's tent in a wooded area, unless he was simply being nosy? I would not be surprised that the guy called the city to complain about a homeless man dwelling on a space where he thinks his dog should be able to play around and not be prevented to urinate on any tree, because a homeless man has set up a tent underneath it. A pet dog can piss on any tree it wants, but a homeless man cannot because in his case, it would have committed a crime called "indecent exposure", even though, the officer who would have arrested him or people who would have complained would have not seen his genitals. I have no understanding of this why can dogs piss on trees and a homeless person who cannot make it to a bathroom can't? If the urine of the dog does not harm the tree, why would that of a human homeless? Also, if a man or a woman cannot afford rent, why is it a problem if he or she puts up a tent on a public space in an area covered by grass and trees and not used as a recreational park, a conservation site, a garden or for any purpose at all, as long as the homeless person who camps there keeps the area clean and does not destroy the environment or endanger the eco-system? No, we can't camp out there because somebody else does not like to drive by or walk by and see a tent sheltering a homeless man on a public space. But when hundreds of homeless men and women sleep on the ground on the sidewalks and sides of the buildings downtown, nobody cares. They rather see a homeless totally deprived and humiliated by sleeping on the ground, even in the freezing winter, than set up a tent in a wooded area that nobody uses but where he can at least keep warm and hold on to his clothes and other possessions and have at least a space to himself and a little dignity with it.

What was I going to do? The idea of going to a shelter was not an option for me to consider. Maybe I should relocate to another spot where my tent will not be visible from the road, I thought. But the only new location I could think of, was a little too dangerous because it was deep in the woods and I see dears coming out of there very often. I don't know what over animals go into that bush at night.

So, I decided to simply take my tent down early in the morning, stash my belongings in the surrounding woods in the day and raise my tent back at night every day. On the weekend, I did not take the tent down from Friday night until Monday morning. I did the same thing every day of the following week, but nobody ever came. The trash that I had piled up eighty feet away by the bridge was still there. I did not take the tent down on the morning of the Monday which followed, because I was running late on my way to take a shower. I stayed out all night that Monday, returned in the morning of Tuesday and slept all day. When I got up at about 4:00 pm to get ready to go back downtown to work on my writings, I heard a car horn blowing. When I stepped out of the tent the black lady from the city's homeless outreach service, called my name. I walked to her car, which was parked by the bridge. She told me that on Thursday, a crew from the city would come to clean the area and remove everything on the premise and in sight including my tent. I told her that I would remove my belongings from there before Thursday morning. Then she told me that, after November 1st, technically, they would not remove me from the place because it was the start of the winter season. So, I did take my tent down every morning and put it back up every night until a day or two after November the 1st. I never moved the tent after that and remained there throughout the winter.

The winter last year was very harsh and there were few snow storms. The ground remained covered with snow for a while. I loved it because I doubted anybody would come and remove my stuff with all the snow on the ground. I prayed that the snow would never melt. A few nights when it was extremely cold outside and the temperature had reached below zero, the city's homeless outreach lady showed up in a van late in the middle of the night and screamed out loud, from the van, that I should come and ride along with them to a warming center. But every time, I told her that I was warm inside and did not need to go to a shelter. I had two sleeping bags and about ten blankets inside my tent and once I got inside both sleeping bags and tossed the blankets on top of me while lying on my mattresses, my body heat kept me warm all night, no matter how cold it got outside.

COLDER IN THE SHELTER THAN IN MY TENT:

One night, after I had stayed in for two straight days because of the incessant rain and snowfall, I decided to step out and go downtown to charge my laptop battery, buy some batteries for my little radio and get some more food.

It was extremely cold but I had to walk all the way to downtown because the Metro bus services were interrupted by the snow storm. I was so cold when I reached downtown. I decided to walk to the Kennedy recreational center because it was used as an emergency warming shelter during the hypothermia weather. I got there by about 4 O'clock because I thought that the center was opened 24 hours a day during hypothermia, but I was there too early because the center opened at 6:00 pm. I did not know what to do next. I needed to go inside a building somewhere to warm up because I was feeling very cold and dizzy and experiencing some headaches. I decided to walk all the way down on Georgia Avenue and hop on the next bus coming my way. But no bus showed up by the time I reached the Harold Washington Convention Center. I entered it on the M street metro station side. A security officer walked towards me as soon as I got inside the building. I told myself that if he ask me to step outside, I would not. When he got closer, I started telling him that I was cold and would leave very soon after I warm up. But he interrupted me and said, "I already know. "Just go sit down and stay for as long as you want" as he pointed to some comfortable sofa in the hall. I sat down and rested for about fifteen minutes until my body warmed up then made my way to the door, although he insisted that I get more rest. But I was starving and tried to make it to the food court at Union Station. I walked down on Massachusetts Avenue to Union Station, charged my laptop's battery and got some to eat there. A couple of hours later, I walked back on Massachusetts Avenue and made a right turn to the Wall mart store on K Street where I purchased some batteries for my radio. From there I walked back to the Kennedy recreational center and got there by 8:00 pm. The gentleman at the desk did a quick intake, handed me a cart and a wool blanket and directed me to a gymnasium where about fifty homeless men were already asleep in the dark. I took the cart out of the box, set it up and tried to go to sleep but I started getting chilly and could not sleep. They had a fan that was turned on and blowing some cold air. I felt colder in the warming center than in my tent. Furthermore, I was shivering and spent the whole night twisting and turning and wishing that I was in my tent because the cart was very uncomfortable unlike the two mattresses in my tent.

In the morning, I walked to SOME House to take a shower and then went to my tent to get more sleep. I regretted the whole experience of going to the hypothermia center.

The next time, when the workers from the homeless outreach drove by and asked me if I wanted to go to the warming center, I said to myself "Hell No! I am fine right here". One morning, while I was about to get up, I heard some noise outside of the tent. I got up about an hour later and checked outside. The deadline on the eviction post was changed to a new date. Now I had until spring to remove my tent and belongings. But I had been there since and no effort had been made by the city to remove me until very recently and curiously in the first week of December. The new Deputy Mayor for Human Services, came by to tell me that new Mayor Muriel Bowser was taking down all homeless encampments in the city and that I should be prepared. That is all she said to me and left. I thought they would not take down any homeless tent in the winter, but I pray that my tent is still there whenever I come back every night until the winter is over.

POPE FRANCIS MOTORCADE RIDING BY MY TENT:

When I heard on the radio that Pope Francis, would visit the basilica at the National shrine on the ground of Catholic University of America, on Wednesday, September 23, 2015, I got worried that for security reasons, the authorities would remove my tent from the vicinity.

But the night before the papal visit to the basilica which is about eight hundred feet from my tent, I stayed out all night and caught the bus back, in the morning. There were roadblocks everywhere in the area, and the bus had to make a detour when it reached the area. The bus driver let me off at about two blocks away from the normal bus stop. I walked up on North Capitol Street and could see from a distance, police cars and tractor trucks blocking the streets by my tent. But, I exhaled and felt relieved, when I reached closer and saw that my tent did not get taken out. I went inside and could see the police cars parked on the middle of the blockaded road and facing me.

While I was watching from inside my tent, I saw few police officers walk to my trash bags by the wall of the bridge and check it probably to make sure there were no bombs or explosives in them. I turned my radio on and tuned to C-span national public radio, because, the whole event at the Basilica was being broadcast live on that station. I felt asleep, but when I woke up by 5:00pm, the police, the trucks and the roadblocks were still in place. I assumed that the Pope was still in the basilica. About an hour later, I saw crowds of people walking down the street from the church. I assumed that the whole thing was over, and the Pope had probably left. But I kept seeing police cars escorting vans, buses and cars on the roads around my tent. Then, I noticed a huge motorcade approaching and heading southbound on North Capitol Street.

I stood in front of my tent, at about eighty feet away, and watched the procession led by motorcycles and cars of secret service and DC metropolitan police. I instinctively assumed that, it was probably the Pope leaving the Basilica on his way to the Vatican Embassy where he was staying during his Washington DC visit. I watched the police motorcycles, cars, armored vehicles and the ambulances and other vehicles in the procession, but I did not see any limousine bearing the flag of the Vatican. I had assumed that this is how I would recognize the vehicle which was transporting Pope Francis. The only vehicle which had the flag of the Vatican in front of it was a tiny little fiat. I thought it was just a regular car in the convoy. I didn't know who was being escorted although it was without a doubt some very important dignitaries.

When I turned the radio back on after I got back into my tent, I heard that the Pope had just left the Basilica into his official vehicle; a small fiat 500 L. Wow, I was so thrilled that Pope Francis had just passed by my tent. He probably saw my tent and me standing in front of it, but I can't say for sure. But I am delighted that he rode by me and that my tent was not removed because of him. He is a good Pope who speaks compassionately about the dispossessed and even had lunch with 300 homeless in Washington DC, on Thursday, September 24, 2015. Hopefully he saw me and prayed for me. Thank you Pope Francis! May God Bless you!

CHAPTER 4:

WHY DON'T YOU GET A JOB?

"Why don't you get a job?" is a question I am frequently asked sometimes with sarcasm followed by statements like "you are a big strong guy and you look intelligent." The assumption with such a statement is that, I must be lazy and not willing to work.

It is evident that many individuals become and stay homeless, because they are making no effort and showing no interest to seek a job, for whatever reasons. There is no question about that. But it is not correct to stereotype all homeless, or even the majority of them as folks who simply are lazy and unwilling to work, but only want to survive on handouts, charities and public assistance.

I love to work. To be honest, I love physical work, although, despite the fact that I am a college drop-out, I consider myself an intellectual. I have done it all like these few examples illustrate.

26 years ago, I worked milking cows at a dairy farm on the campus of the college that I attended in Michigan in 1989. I did quit after few weeks, because I was tired of smelling like cow dungs that I had to clean every night after milking the cows. My next job was at a bakery on the same campus, where I was greasing pans, which were used to bake cakes. A year later, I left for Oklahoma where I had transferred to a cheaper school. I got a part-time cleaning job on the campus of the college in Oklahoma, plus another part-time office cleaning job outside of campus. I later got a job at a nursing home where I was cleaning old folks' rooms. Then when I left Oklahoma to Washington D.C, I did work at a Kentucky Fried Chicken in Hyattsville, Maryland, where I was frying chicken.

Then, when I left the chicken-frying job, I got a job as a sales representative at a tour company in D.C. I later did some labor at construction sites with temp agencies. I am therefore not allergic to work. Whenever I went to a job for a labor agency or a subcontractor, I was requested to come back because I always worked hard. Although it is true that most of the menial jobs, that I have worked, did not generate enough income to afford a place to live and take care of daily needs, I still could rent a room in a rooming house when many of them used to be available.

But things have changed since. In D.C, rooming houses are things of the past, and the few people who rent rooms out, charge as much, if not more than the cost of renting a one bedroom apartment. Years ago, when many people used to turn their houses into rooming houses, the rooms averagely rented from $300 to $500. Today, if there is any room advertised in the Washington post, the average rent would range from $800 to over a $1,000.

So, the reason why I have not had any living wage employment is not because I do not like to work, but instead because I worked menial jobs most of the time. But to be honest, having learned how to survive out there and worked for other people for little money, I am more tempted to start my own business in a near future. I am not sure in what specific field, but I have learned from the streets how to be entrepreneurial. I will explain.

HOMELESS ENTREPRENEUR:

It was a cold month of December 1998. I was staying inside a trailer at Randall Shelter in Ivy City, in North East Washington DC. I had a cold and was not feeling too well. I noticed few of the guys that I knew waking up around 4 o'clock early in the morning, and heard them mention that they were going downtown and make some money. When few of them returned to the shelter that night, I asked them where they did go to make money so early in the morning and how. One explained to me that, they did go to line up to get free Van Gogh tickets for some scalpers at the National Gallery of art. The scalpers would pay each of them $5 per ticket for the maximum four free tickets per person give-away inside the Museum. Well, I thought that I could go and get some of these free tickets and try to sell them myself for at least $10 each and make $40. I heard one of them say that he sold his tickets outside the venue to visitors of the museum who could not get free tickets. So, the next morning, I also got up at 4:00 am and walked down to the National Art Gallery Museum with the other homeless guys.

Once I got there, I found out what was going on. The National Gallery -located on the National Mall- was holding an exhibition of the famous paintings of the renowned Dutch painter Vincent Van Gogh, in collaboration with the Van Gogh Museum in Amsterdam where they are originally conserved. But a set of tickets with a limit of four tickets per person, was freely given out at the Museum every day starting at 8:00 am, for the period of time that the exhibition was taking place in Washington DC. The number of visitors to the museum for the exhibition probably doubled or sometimes tripled the number of available tickets. So those who showed up early, had a better chance of getting tickets, on a first come first served basis. Since it was the only chance for Vincent Van Gogh's art aficionados in the U.S to see his masterpieces, because it was the only exhibition of the kind in the U.S, they flocked by the thousands and came from as far as New York City and beyond, to get a chance to see them.

As the exhibition were drawing to its end, the best chance to get a ticket was to camp in line outside the museum, as early as midnight or 1:00 am. Few ingenious scalpers had the astute idea of recruiting some homeless men and women to hold a spot in a ticket line, late in the night and very early in the morning, and get four free tickets each. Each of them then turned in his or her four tickets to the scalpers in exchange for $5 to $10 for each ticket. The scalpers resold the tickets few hours later for sometimes $50 to $100 apiece to desperate visitors who showed up later in the day and realized that the Museum had ran out of free tickets for the day.

When I got there and understood what was going on, I waited for a couple of hours after I got my first tickets and sold them outside the museum for $20 apiece. I made $80 that day. I returned later in the night and lined up by 3:00 am because people who joined the line after 6:00 am had a very unlikely chance to get tickets.

I had just found out that the exhibition had lasted for over a month and was in its last week. I wished I had known about it sooner because I would have made a lot of money. I decided to come out there every night for that last week until the last day. On the second day, I offered to another homeless guy that I knew, $40 for his four tickets, although he had lined up for another scalper who was buying his tickets for $5 apiece. He agreed.

I therefore, had 8 tickets this time around and sold all of them for at least $20 each and one or two for a little more. I noticed few other homeless trying to sell their tickets themselves out there but were not doing very well because of the competition from others and the fear of being caught by the park police officers. So, I offered some of them $20 for their four tickets when it was obvious to me that they were getting impatient, desperate and in a hurry to leave. It was also a way for me to get them out of the way and return later, when there were a lot of people out there looking for tickets and very few people selling them. I made three to four hundred dollars the second day and more and more each day until the last day. I ended up with a couple of thousand dollars when the exhibition ended. It was a blessing.

I found out that the scalpers who brought the homeless to line up and get tickets for them at the Van Gogh Exhibit were professionals who did the same at venues where tickets for concerts or other entertainment shows were going on sale.

I also found out that they were making a lot of money at local sports venues. So when the 2003 NBA basketball season started, I went to the MCI Center-now the Verizon Center- to see if I could make a few bucks by replicating the Van Gogh ticket experience. Most of the same scalpers plus many others were selling mostly season tickets that they got at cheaper cost while on sale. I watched them buy extra tickets from the fans for less than the tickets cost and reselling them for more. I used the little money I had and did the same thing. I was lucky to find someone who will take, let's say, $20 for a ticket which had a face value price of $80 dollars for example, and resold it for more than I spent for it.

Some nights I made great profits, but many other nights, I took losses. When the games were not sold-out and tickets were still available at the ticket booths, we were sometimes forced to sell our tickets for lower than the face value and even for lower than we had gotten them. Only those who had great seats' tickets were lucky to sell them for a little more than they had spent to get them.

In addition to scalping tickets, I also made money on rainy days by purchasing umbrellas at Farmers Market off Florida Avenue, North East Washington DC, at wholesale price for $20 a dozen. I sold them for $5 apiece at Metro stations in the District of Columbia, mainly at China Town Gallery place, McPherson and DuPont Circle stations. First, I used to buy a dozen or two, depending on how much money I had on me, when I knew from the weather forecast in the newspaper that it was going to rain incessantly the next day or couple of days.

In conclusion, I have no problem working as I have evidenced in the few examples I gave. Sometimes, circumstances that we do not control can prevent us from working at times, and sometimes, for a long period of time. But there is always hope for those who do not give up and keep trying to overcome the worse of difficulties.

CHAPTER 5:

Exploitation of the homeless

The homeless are a very vulnerable population who, and whose conditions, are exploited by unscrupulous people, as I would illustrate through the following examples: It is comprehensible and even unobjectionable that people out there who may have a place to call home and even a job but who are just as needy, impoverished or flat broke as the homeless, join them at soup kitchens or other places to get free meals and handouts. I have seen regular well dressed pedestrians line up to get a plate when they noticed folks serving home cooked meals to the homeless. Most of the time, they either did not realize that it was free food served to homeless people.

Or they knew but were hungry and not able to afford a meal and probably did not have enough food at home. This is also most likely the case of some black school kids and other pedestrians, who, on their way to the train and bus stations nearby, line up for a meal served to the homeless in front the church and headquarters of Catholic Charities of America -right across The Martin Luther King Library-, every Wednesday afternoon, from 5:00pm to 6:00pm.

But, it is not right for people, who are neither deprived nor homeless, to pretend to be homeless or needy and go around the city to collect and make lucrative use of charitable goods that are exclusively offered to the homeless to help and assist them.

Unfortunately, such fake-homeless exist in Washington DC, and guess who they are?

FAKE CHINESE HOMELESS CHASING HAND-OUTS:

Every Saturday and Sunday, dozens of churches, charitable groups and compassionate individuals bring tons of foods, clothes, hygiene items, and handouts in Franklin Park all day long. I made it a habit to go there every weekend to get supplies of water bottles, soaps, toothpastes, canned-food and other goods that I save in my tent and use when I have to stay in. Many former homeless men and women and other poor folks who live in low-income housing come there also to collect handouts to take home for personal use.

Honest truth, most of the homeless that I see in Washington D.C are in majority; blacks (mostly African-Americans but also many from Africa and the Caribbean Islands), a good number of whites, a lot of Hispanics, few Asians and rarely few Europeans, mostly from Russia and Eastern Europe. For some reasons, it is extremely rare to see homeless who are nationals of some of the wealthiest countries of Western Europe or Asia unless they are mentally ill. I have never seen any German, Swedish, Swiss, Japanese, Saudi Arabian homeless in America. It was therefore a shock when I noticed a group of a dozen and more old Chinese men and women literally run towards every truck, group, church, car, bus, van or individual showing up with donations, food and goods for the homeless, to the amazement of the homeless themselves. "Ain't no way, these people are homeless," I told myself. I have been into Chinatown billion times for the past 10 years and I have never seen any Chinese homeless. I have never seen them in homeless shelters either, and I doubt there are that many poor Chinese in Washington DC. They are averagely a very successful group of people with a strong sense of community and they help one another. So, I started getting curious and skeptical because I just could not believe that these 60 and 70 year old Chinese men and women would be abandoned by their well-to-do children who are business owners, doctors, lawyers etc., to the point that, they would have to come get food donated for the homeless. I found the whole thing fishy.

So, I observed them and found out that, they showed up in the park at, as early as 6:00 am and stayed there till 5:00 pm every Saturday and Sunday. And the curious thing about them is that, each of them brings a shopping cart, a backpack on their back and a shopping bag in their hands.

All of them reside in two apartment buildings few blocks away: The Wah Luck Building on 6th and H Streets and the Congress square complex on 5th and K Streets, North-West. They walk in group from their apartment buildings to the park and store their shopping carts on the northeastern end of the park, in the custody of one Hispanic homeless man who keeps his belongings and sleeps there every night on a blanket. I don't know if they pay him for keeping an eye on their loot, but he has been doing this for at least a year since I have been observing them. As soon as they see a car, a van or a person bring stuff to the homeless in the park, they sprint towards the givers, fill their handbags and backpacks with handouts, take them back and empty everything into their cart then return right back to get more handouts. They do that back and forth all day long. As soon as their shopping carts are filled up, one lady among them who seems to be supervising the group, makes a phone call to someone who drives to the park to pick up the spoils.

Many times, the homeless men and women in the park have expressed their frustration at the old Chinese folks because they are very greedy and aggressive. "They grab, grab, grab" as one old Hispanic lady who always complains about them, likes to say, when she warns the people from churches and other charitable groups who hand out stuff in the park.

I heard many of the homeless complain that, the old Chinese folks were getting the stuff to sell them. I even was told by two homeless men that they had seen one of them selling the stuff at a makeshift vending stand that he had outside of Union Station. One morning, I saw him myself set up his vending stand by a construction site on K and 7th Streets. That was enough evidence for me. I also heard other homeless folks say that they have seen them sell the stuff in Chinatown on the street outside of the Wah Luck building where some of them live. It is very obvious to me that these old Chinese folks are being organized by some folks in the Washington D.C Chinese business community who collect the goods probably in exchange for few bucks and make a lucrative use of them. I will not be surprised that these goods end up on the shelves of some Chinese stores in the DC, Maryland and Virginia region.

The normal and average homeless men or women in the park normally take things that they need, but the old Chinese scavengers take as much as they can of everything that can be sold. I give an example. Many of the folks who bring food and handouts to the park, bring bottles of water. The average homeless takes a few bottles of water to consume right away in the park or for later. But the old Chinese folks take every bottle of water that they can put their hands on. So, by the end of the day, each of them collects up to 30 of 40 bottles of water. If you multiply 40 bottles of water by 20 Chinese men and women, you have 800 bottles of water that they take out of the park collectively on a Saturday and 800 more on Sunday. In addition to bottles of water, they collect tons of bars of soaps, bottles of lotion and shampoos, soda cans, food cans, T-shirts, thermos garments, boots, jackets, blankets and gifts cards from 6:00 am to 6:00 pm every Saturday and Sunday.

The good people, organizations and Churches sincerely don't know that they are also supplying Chinese vendors and stores in the Washington D.C area, when they hand their donations to these old Chinese men and women who mingle among the homeless every weekend in the park. What really worries me is that I have no idea what they do with the cooked meals they collect, and I will not be surprised if parts and pieces of these meals end up in Chinese restaurants in Chinatown. I am saying this because I have seen the old Chinese folks get plates of cooked meals, remove pieces of chicken out of them and dump the rest in the trash. I know one thing, I no longer and will never eat at any Chinese Restaurant in Chinatown, because I have no idea whether the pieces of chicken on any plate in these restaurants, come from plates distributed to the homeless at Franklin Park or not.

Another evidence that they are organized by a mob of Chinese merchants is that, they show up as a group - with each of them carrying a backpack- at many of the places where there is a distribution of handouts to the homeless. For example, every 4th Sunday of the month, they show up at Asbury United Methodist Church, at 926 11th Street, NW, where toiletries and undergarments are given out to the homeless after breakfast from 9:00 am to 10:30 am. Even the people of the church know that these old Chinese people are not homeless. But the church people do not know what to do when they see them come in as if there were coming to a restaurant, and sit down to be served the breakfast normally intended for the homeless, then line up to get the stuff that are also normally intended to be given to the homeless. They even notice some of the old Chinese folks trying to get back in line and get more stuff, but they pull them off the line. One day, I noticed a lady among them, who speaks English fluently, tell the old Chinese men in the line to ask for size Large, when they get inside the room where long johns were being distributed to the homeless. To the exception of a very few, all of them were short and barely around 5 foot tall on average and could only fit small to medium sizes. But

83

I guess whoever was collecting all these thermal undergarments sold more size L. It is a shame that some Chinese merchants have made of collecting donations to the homeless, a lucrative business and are using their granddads and grandmas as fake-homeless. But the weirdest part of it all is the churches that come to serve food and give handouts to the homeless in Franklin Park are White churches from Virginia or West-Virginia for most, African-American churches from Maryland or the District, Hispanic churches, African churches, Korean churches, even Vietnamese churches and churches with mixed ethnic membership. But I have never seen a Chinese Church show up at the park. I wonder how the old Chinese fake homeless grandpas and grandmas would react if a church of their own community showed up at the park and saw them collecting handouts that they use as supplies for their stores and businesses. Last but not the least, sometimes they show up with their American-born grand kids in the park. These kids probably live and go to school in upper and middle class neighborhoods in Virginia. They are dropped by their parents to their grand-parents in DC who take them to the park while babysitting them. I watched these English-speaking American-born Chinese kids and noticed how tensed, annoyed and uncomfortable they were when their grandparents dragged them to line up with the homeless to grab handouts. I wonder if, when they returned home, they ever told their parents about being taken to the park by grandma and grandpa to hang out and chase handouts with the homeless.

UNSCRUPULOUS DENTISTS:

If I had not been homeless myself, I could have never imagined how vulnerable to exploitation by unscrupulous people the homeless population were.

I will start with a simple example. Many mentally or physically disable homeless receive social security benefits and medical assistance. Some dentists in the Washington D.C region figured out that they could generate a lot of money for their business from the government by offering $20 to homeless men and women, to come and get their teeth cleaned or get dental work done, in their clinic. I was filling some forms at the waiting room to see the dentist at the clinic for the homeless at SOME. I noticed this guy who was not a worker there but was trying to be very discrete as he approached some of the homeless in the waiting room and told them that he could help them make $20 cash if they had Medicaid. I was really curious to know why this scoundrel would come inside the clinic and try to get some of the patients who were there to see the dentist, to go to another clinic and be paid $20 for the same free dental work, which they were about to receive.

Many other times, I saw the same person standing outside of SOME, and telling any homeless man or woman who passed him on their way to get some breakfast, that if they had Medicaid they could make $20.

There is also another homeless man who comes inside the father Mc Kenna center, walks around the place and shouts: "if you have Medicaid, I will help you make $20 right now". "Doing what?" Some curious homeless men do answer back. And he tells them: "I will take you to the dentist, they will clean your teeth or do some dental work on you if you need any, and you will be paid $20. "If you want to make some money now, instead of sitting here all day and stay broke, I will call my man now and he will come and pick us up. "You need to have a picture ID and your Medicaid card". Then few guys who were interested, would say: "I need some money. I can use that $20," The guy then tries to get as many homeless men as he can, then he calls the office of the dentist for whom he is hustling, to have them send a drive. Most of the time, he gets two or three guys, although more than often, no one falls for the offer. Obviously, he was receiving commissions for doing this. Evidently the homeless are easy prey to these dentists who pay them $20 but charge the government hundreds of dollars for services that their homeless victim is probably overcharged for. It would have been fair to pay the homeless man at least $300 instead of $20 for a service that the dentist charges the government $600 for example. But these unscrupulous dentists won't do that because the whole thing is a fraud anyway. Here is how this illegal activity is define in Wikipedia: "In the United States, Medicare fraud is the collection of Medicare health care reimbursement under false pretenses. There are many different types of Medicare fraud, all of which have the same goal: to collect money from the Medicare program illegitimately." SLUMLORDS:

A homeless man who got an apartment paid by some social services, invited his homeless friend to move in with him. His friend who I knew on the streets took me to the apartment and asked him to let me stay there for a few bucks a week, which I was willing to pay. He accepted and I moved in and was paying him $10 every day. He was a 70 year old alcoholic and a very friendly man who spent most of his time drinking on the streets and did not come in to the apartment for a couple of weeks. A few times, I found him drunk on the streets and asked him to come home, but he looked at me and asked me if I was OK in the apartment. I told him that I was and begged him to come home. But he told me that he was alright right there on the ground in the park, and would sleep outside. But when the winter approached and when his other friend started coming in, he progressively started coming home. His friend brought in his girlfriend, so we were altogether four people in the apartment. Nobody else but I was paying him to stay there, although, anytime I walked to him every morning to give him the $10, he kept insisting that I did not have to give him anything. But I insisted that he takes the money because he needed it to a least get some to eat. And also, I stayed there by myself for two months and did not pay anything, although I gave him some money whenever I saw him on the street. So, I made sure that while he was in the apartment, he had some money to get some to eat at least.

His friends who were staying in the house did not care to make sure that he gets anything to eat. They only offered him some liquor and anytime he had any money, they took it from him to buy alcohol. The apartment had one bedroom and I was staying in it. His friends used the dining room as their bedroom and he was sleeping in the couch in the living room. The apartment was located in a four unit apartment building in the Trinidad neighborhood. All the apartments in the building were rented by former homeless men who were getting their rent paid through government housing assistance voucher for low-income residents, also known as section 8. The landlord was a young black lady in her thirties. All the three other apartments were well kept unlike the one we were staying in. There was a hole in the floor of the bedroom by the side of the wall, and from my bed, I could see the ground outside underneath the building. The bathroom sink stayed broken. The maintenance guy came regularly to fix it by only putting a piece of wood stick underneath to hold and prevent it from collapsing to the ground. The closets had mildew all over their walls. The water in the apartment was heated by an old gas tank water heater which, one day, exploded and created a sizable crater in the kitchen's old wood floor. The building was not secured because the front door lock was not working. Late at night, male and female drug addicts used to push the door open and engage in crack cocaine smoking and sex in the stairway.

Until I left the place, the landlord never fixed anything despite the numerous complaints about maintenance and safety regularly brought to her attention. Yet, she was still cashing on money paid by the government for rent in the poorly maintained apartments and unsafe building. The guy ultimately used his housing voucher to move to a better apartment in another part of town.

I had my own personal past experience with slumlords. At one time, I was renting a room at a rooming house at the intersection of Florida Avenue and 3rd Street, Northwest for only $75 a week. The place was a mess and not suitable for human habitation. The building was decayed and infested with rodents. When I was in my bed at night with the lights turned off, I could hear the rats moving and squeaking around in my room, in the kitchen, in the hallway and in every other parts of the building.

One day, as soon as I opened the front door of the building downstairs, a rat sprang to the staircase from outside right up in front of me and sprinted upstairs. Another day, I came home and turned on the light downstairs but there was no electricity in the building. I walked upstairs in the dark and was informed by the guy who occupied the first room by the stairs that there had been an electric fire in the building earlier. The firemen had punched a hole in the roof above my room in order to get to the top of the building through my room. The door was wide open when I walked in. I found debris scattered everywhere and all over my bed and could see the sky through the huge hole above my bed. Nobody cared to clean the mess and cover the hole in the roof. I had to go outside to find some plywood and cardboards, and cover it myself.

The landlord or slumlord should I rather say, collected the rent every Friday during the whole month that we were deprived of electricity. The hole in my roof was not fixed until I moved to the room next door a month later, when it was vacated by its renter.

Obviously he knew that finding cheap rooms, like his, in the city was hard. Besides, I, as well as all the other renters were homeless who were fortunate to have him rent us a room, although we had no stable source of income.

I eventually left the place in the winter when day labor jobs became scarce. I had no money to pay the rent sometimes. When I came home one Friday night, my door had a padlock on it because I was a week late on my rent. So the only way I could get inside my room was to come and see the landlord in the morning when he came to his very nasty rat-infested restaurant which was located at the bottom of the building. I used to wonder, who was crazy enough to go eat there. But, I just left that night and never returned, not only because I had no money to pay him, but also because I was tired of living in a filthy place and being pressured to pay rent when I was a week late. Also, I had paid rent for a whole month for a room without electricity and with a hole in the roof. Whatever happened to my belongings is everybody's guess. I was back on the streets as a homeless again and lost all my possessions.

HOMELESS, EXPLOITED AS CHEAP LABOR:

The stereotype that homeless are lazy and don't want to work is not true. So many homeless men and women get up as early as 5 o'clock every morning to go to work for day labor agencies and sub-contractors. But they are taken advantage of by being overworked and underpaid, sometimes below minimum wage.

As many homeless men seeking day jobs do every morning, I used to wait at the corner of 2nd and D streets by the CCNV Shelter for any truck seeking day laborers to pull over so I could go and make me a few bucks for the day. "Leo! My man is about to pull up" said, a homeless man, who I knew and will only identify as E. E had just talked to a Nigerian sub-contractor who used to come and pick him up every morning and have him find few hard working men to go work with them. "What y'all be doin'?" I asked him. "We be movin' stores and kitchen equipment" He answered. "It is some hard work, you want to go?" He added. "No problem," I responded. "How much he pays?" was my next question. "$40 for the day," he answered. Few minutes later, a pick-up van pulled up and E gathered the guys that he had picked. I was new but all the other guys were regulars. The man let me get on the truck after he asked me if I could handle hard work and I assured him that I could.

We were six guys riding with him. He drove us to somewhere in Maryland where we picked commercial kitchen equipment, loaded them on the van and unloaded them at several restaurants in other parts of Maryland.

I never lifted anything so heavy in my life. After doing this all day for no less than 8 hours, the man asked me if I could be back the next day. He appreciated the work I did and assured me that I could work for him anytime. Actually he paid me $50, while he paid E and the other guys $40.

$50 or $40 for lifting these 600 and more pounds of steel and heavy metal stuff all day was not fair at all. I was desperate for the money but not too sure if I wanted to subject myself to such an ill treatment. I was sleeping outside at the time. When I woke up early in the morning about 5:00 am, I could barely get up because my body was so sore. I decided that I was in too much pain to go back to kill myself for 8 hours for only $50. It was not worth it, I concluded. So I did not go.

Few days later, I went back to the same spot, but jumped on a truck of a guy (let's call him S) who had his own moving company and was picking up guys to go do moving jobs. Unlike me, all the guys who jumped on the truck had worked with him before. He asked me if I had done moving jobs before. My answer was negative. But he let me go anyway. I ended up enjoying the job. Anytime he showed up at the shelter, I was outside ready to go. Although he was paying us very little money despite the hard work we put in, I still liked the job. Most of the people that we moved, added a tip for the workers to the amount that he or she was being billed by the moving company owner. But S kept the tips and just paid us only for our labor. Some of the workers who were discontented with such exploitative practice, privately approached the customers and told them that if they had any intention to tip us, they should give it directly to us instead of the boss because he would keep it for himself.

Many times, the moving company owner sent me and a couple of other guys, to do jobs in different states by ourselves. We made good money from tips on these jobs. At one job, the client approached me while I was by myself and told me that, I was working very hard compared to the three other guys. He gave me a $100 tip and advised me to think about starting my own moving company one day. On another job that I was sent to with another guy on a Sunday morning, I was the only one who showed up. The other guy was missing in action. I called the boss who was on another job far from the area. I was doing the job in Alexandria, Virginia and not far from a Metro Station. The boss was located in Baltimore Maryland. He had instructed me to try to do the job by myself and collect the check of $500, and bring it to him the next day, when he picks me up at the shelter for another job. I unloaded the truck by myself, loaded all the furniture and the stuff on the apartment building's freight elevator, took them upstairs and carried everything piece by piece to the apartment. The customers- a wife and her husband- were very upset that I had to do all the job by myself, while they had been billed for a two workers' job. Then the wife told her husband to write the check to my name instead of the company's, because she thought that it was not fair that I did a job by myself to be paid only $40 by the boss, who was billing them $500, although he did not send two workers as they agreed. But I told them that, I could not keep the $500, because I would no longer be able to work for the same dude. So, they wrote him instead a $300 check and gave me $200 in cash for myself. I lied to him that they did not give me any tip because they were upset. He paid me $50 for that job. I could go on with more examples to show how I have done hard work as a slave labor out of desperation.

But the truth of the matter is that many homeless who are desperate for cash money are exploited every day on day jobs where they work very hard and are paid very less.

EVICTIONS:

Every morning, eviction companies pick up homeless men and women outside of shelters and soup kitchens and pay them barely anything to go and move out of apartments and houses, the belongings of men, women or families who are being evicted in the presence of U.S Marshalls in Washington D.C or county Sheriffs in Maryland. Most of the homeless go out to do evictions all day for sometimes less than $30 a day and have to wait for hours to get their money, many a time.

Many of them are incentivized by the prospect of being able to thieve some of the evicted people's jewelry, electronics and other valuables to make up for the low wage they receive for the jobs.

I used to go on eviction jobs with only one and the same eviction company driver - I will identify as D- because he was like a friend to me, and would allow me to go into rooms, where they were most likely some good stuff to find. It is no secret in the eviction world that crews and their supervisors and even some of the police officers on site, pocket cash money and keep valuables that they find on the job, when the person being evicted is not present and have an apartment or house full of valuables and sometimes cash money.

I wondered why certain people were getting evicted since they had very expensive furniture, electronics, clothing and jewelry; and why they did not move their valuables out before the evictions. Was it possible that they had died, were incarcerated or hospitalized and had nobody

95

who could retrieve and secure their belongings? Or were they simply negligent and did not expect the eviction to take place while they were away, at work, on a trip or hospitalized? I was even dumbfounded to see or hear about so much cash that was found in some of the evicted homes.

We did an apartment in Maryland where the evicted lady who was absent had closets filed with no less than two hundred pairs of shoes and so much clothes, which could be used to open a store.

D asked me to go in one of the bedroom and directed the others to the living room, kitchen and bathroom. He himself went to work in some of the closets and part of the living room where he knew he could come across some good stuff. When I entered the bedroom, the Sheriff who was in there, had pulled a lot of cash money from some drawers. I was pretending not to pay attention to him, but I watched him pocket $5, $10 and $20 bills and discard one dollar bills on the bed. When he left the room, I approached the bed and gathered about 25 dollar bills off it. I assumed that he had purposely left the dollar bills on the bed for me; so I just picked up the money and put it in my pocket. It took us at least three hours to move all the stuff from the apartment and sit it on the sidewalk. The person who lived there never showed up. Everybody on the crew found something valuable that they could either keep or sell on the street, whether it was jewelry or something else. At the end of the job, D himself discretely took out a card box full of stuff and sat it in the front of the truck by his side, before he drove off.

We got paid only $5 for that job which took us three hours of packing and moving out furniture, bags of clothes, and all kind of household stuff in addition to trash. At that time, most eviction companies were paying only $5 per job for an apartment and $10 for a house. But when they had sometimes 10 to 20 evictions scheduled in a day at various apartment complexes in the city of Washington and in the Maryland suburbs, they only paid the homeless laborers $35 for the day because it was a so-called package deal. Although many of the apartments were walk-throughs -meaning that the renters had already moved out all their belongings and left nothing inside but some little trash-, some others were packed.

We did not get paid for travel time although we travelled for an hour from the soup kitchen to the job site and waited, sometimes for one hour or two, for the U.S Marshall in Washington D.C, or the County Sheriff in Maryland to show up and carry out the evictions. This means that we made only five dollar for the day, if we had only one job scheduled for that day, or other scheduled jobs were cancelled because the people to be evicted made payment at the last minute.

After the job or jobs were done for the day, the driver had to drive to a gas station somewhere in Landover, Maryland to wait to get paid by his boss who took sometimes a couple of hours before showing up.

Imagine this: A homeless man who got picked up at SOME early in the morning around 7:30 am without eating breakfast- because the eviction van had to leave before breakfast was served- and travelled for an hour to the job site, then waited for two hours for the police to show up, did a couple of jobs for two hours, then went to wait for two more hours to get paid and finally returned to the city by 4:00 pm, with only $10 pay for the day.

When the homeless are being exploited like that every day on eviction jobs, how can they be blamed when they pocket whatever valuable they found on the job? Off course, because they are being victimized by those who hire them to do the eviction does not give them the right to victimize those who are being evicted. I am by no means excusing the thievery going on during evictions.

Here is one more story. One day D took us to a job in Georgetown which is an affluent neighborhood of Washington D.C. We had to evict a pizza parlor on M street where most of the stores and restaurants in Georgetown are located. The U.S Marshalls showed up few minutes after we had got there. Also, a city trash removal truck and workers were present to remove immediately from the street all the stuff to be evicted from the store. When we got to the store, D sent me to a room in the back of the store and two guys to another isolated room, while the rest of the guys were asked to remove the stuff in the dining room. The two guys who were sent to the other room stumbled upon an unlocked cash register. The smarter of the two asked his accomplice to stand by the door and be on the lookout while he pocketed the loot.

Nobody knew how much money was in the cash register, but the guy at the register stuffed his jacket and undergarments with big bills and discarded some of the one-dollar bills in a trash bag. He closed the cash register, left the room and alerted the U.S Marshalls of the presence of a cash register in the room, after he had stashed enough money in his clothing.

The Marshalls went in the room, seized the cash register and counted and took custody of the rest of the money. They did not check the two guys to find out if they had subtracted some money out of the cash register before leaving the room.

When the eviction was completed, we got back in the van and sat against each side of the van because there were no seats in the back. The guy who took the money out of the cash register was hysterical while patting his jacket full of money.

His partner in crime was gesturing to him in a clear indication that he was expecting his share the loot. D, the driver looked in the rear view mirror and asked the lucky guy to share some of the money with him. The guy gave him about $200 and also gave some money to the other guy, but I did not see how much. D asked him how much he had got from the register. The guy claimed that he did not know exactly how much he pocketed. Did he get a couple of thousands of dollars? Nobody knew because he never said. But he told his accomplice that he had stacked a lot of one dollar bills in one of the plastic bag that he had passed to him, because he was hoping that the guy would ask someone to take it to the van so that the rest of us could share the money. Unfortunately, the trash bag was handed to one of the city trash truck employee who tossed it on the back of the trash truck without knowing that there was money inside. We had to go to another job, but the guy who had found the money got off the van about five blocks away without even asking for his pay. We got paid $10 for the job. I wished I was the one in the room where the cash register was. But I don't know if I would have had the guts to stuff myself with so much money and then tell the police that there was a cash register in the room.

In conclusion, I want to stress the fact that so many homeless men and women out there are working or willing to work their ass off, but unscrupulous employers who understand their desperation take advantage of them by overworking and underpaying them.

CHAPTER 6:

THE WEIRDEST THINGS I HAVE SEEN OUT THERE

Some of the weirdest things that I have seen in my life have happened within the homeless community. Few examples; The case of the homeless man who refuses any food that is handed to him but eats only food that he picks out of trash cans. Or the case of the other homeless man that I have seen throwing a $20 bill back at a couple who walked by him and deposited the money next to him while he was lying down about to go to sleep by the side of a building. But these cases can be attributed to dementia or other severe mental illnesses. But, the four extremely weird cases on the top of my list are extraordinarily exceptional situations I ever witnessed.

THE CHARITABLE NYMPH:

About 15 years ago, in the year 2000 to be precise, I was about to lose a room that I was renting in a rooming house. Because I was homeless off and on, all my friends with whom I was spending my time were homeless who were sleeping in back alleys, parks or shelters. One of my close friends told me that he was awaken by a lady one night while he was asleep in a church doorway adjacent to a little park on New York Avenue, about two blocks from the White House. It was the end of fall and the start of winter. She was a 5'5 attractive young black brown-skinned lady probably in her early 30's.

When he woke up, she stood in front of him pretending to be looking for a person by a name she made up. He said that she wore an unbuttoned fur coat and was totally naked under it. She then asked him if he wanted sex. I leave what happened next to the reader's imagination. After that first appearance, she showed up several other times and did the same to other homeless men sleeping in the same spot. No one knew exactly when she would show up, but they knew that at least twice a week she would show up like a ghost and surprise them in their sleep. At first, it was hard for me to believe that a normal and good looking woman would go around the city, wake up homeless men and offer them free sex. I can imagine that charitable peoples and organizations who care for the homeless, come out to offer them food, clothes, even money or services whether medical, legal or housing assistance. But it never crossed my mind that a young attractive lady will offer gratuitous sexual gratification to the homeless as an act of charity. I decided to sleep in the back-alley in the same garage space with my homeless buddies, the Saturday night when I finally lost my room at the rooming house. In the middle of the night, at around 2:00 am, I felt somebody kicking my feet while I was in a deep sleep. When I opened my eyes, my friend pointed at a lady who was standing between him and me. Here she is, he told me. That was "pussy girl" as we had nicknamed her since nobody ever knew her name. I was dumbstruck and could see her nakedness under her fur coat. He gesticulated to assure her that she could trust me. Did I succumb or did I resist? I will keep the suspense by not answering the question.

But something was very strange about her. She did not engage in a conversation and would even leave when any of the guy tried to press or converse with her. She chose whoever she wanted to have sex with and did have sex with two, or three guys one after the other. Or sometimes she came discretely, woke up one homeless man, had sex with him while the others were sleeping, left and returned and hour or two later to have sex with another guy and back and forth, until she had sex with everybody that was willing to copulate with her that night. When some of the guys politely told her that they were not interested when she woke them up, she went ahead and woke up the next man until someone accepted. Sometimes, she returned the same night and tried to have sex again with the guys that she had sex with hours earlier.

I learned later from other homeless men who were beneficiaries of her charitable sexual service that whichever night she was coming out, she used to go to various parks, back alleys, church steps and anywhere to service homeless men wherever she could find them sleeping, in the middle of the night. All of them said that she used the same astuteness by first approaching them, waking them up and asking them if they wanted sex for free. She was not a prostitute and she refused any money that some of the homeless that she approached for the first time offered her.

Another peculiar thing about her is that she had a bodyguard who escorted her to the alleys or isolated places where she was hunting for homeless men. But he used to walk away without interfering with what she was doing, but stayed in comfortable distance to protect her from harm and alert her in case. When she finished, they walked to their van and drove away. Sometimes she was driving, but other times, he was behind the wheel. They used to spend the entire night doing this, starting from around midnight till dawn.

One night I noticed her minivan parked in a parking space in front of a church on K and 9th Streets. I saw her and her bodyguard coming out and she walked up the steps of the church while he waited at the bottom. There was one homeless man sleeping up there by himself. Few minutes later, I saw her walking back down the steps and get in the van with her bodyguard. When they drove away, I walked up the Church steps and asked the homeless man who was sleeping on the terrace, what happened. He looked dazed. He had never seen or heard of her before, and never expected anything like that ever.

He told me that she came up the steps, woke him up and asked him if he wanted sex but he responded that he had no money. She assured him that she did not want money. He told her, "but where we gonna do it?" "Right here" she responded. "But this is the Church" he retorted. He refused to have sex with her on the church ground, despite her attempt to reassure him that it was ok to do it there. That was about five years ago. I have never seen or heard about her again since.

INDIAN GHOST LADY:

The first night at my spot, I stretched out on the ground on a blanket with the tarp underneath it because I had not set up my tent yet. But I woke up instinctively, when I sensed a presence in the dark about hundred feet away. I stared in the direction of the silhouette under the tree but could not discern what the thing was.

I got a little afraid and thought it could be a wild animal that was stalking me in the dark. I grasped the iron pole that I had tucked under my blanket to use as protection. But I was surprised to see a woman getting up in a posture which suggested that she was urinating on the tree. She became more identifiable as she walked closer to me. She was a chubby big-breasted 5 foot tall lady. She wore a white T-shirt, some sweatpants and some tennis shoes. She had long dark hair, a light brown complexion and looked like she had origins from the Indian Peninsula, although she spoke English with a perfect American accent. Before I said anything to her, she asked me why I was homeless. It was about 2:00 am. I responded, "What are you doing here that late in the dark?" She did not want to answer at first and insisted that I tell her my story. She asked me whether she could sit on my blanket, I told her no problem. I told her that I would tell her my story, but she had to explain to me first who she was and why she was out there that late. "Do you live in the area"? I asked her. "Yes, but no more" she answered. "What you mean no more?" I asked her. She told me that she was not going to go back home anymore, and that, she was God and was going to live like Jesus, and wander from place to place to save the poor and people who dwell outside. At that moment it was clear to me that she was mentally ill and was having an episode. I tried to convince her to return home wherever she lived at, but it was a waste of my time. She insisted instead that, I tell her my story and that she had come to save me. But she got mad because I said no, when she asked me whether I believed that she was God.

She walked away from me and headed towards the north of North Capitol Street in the dark. I got worried because some mischievous driver could kidnap her off the dark road which was surrounded by bushes. I felt asleep as soon as she left. Moments later, I jumped off my sleep because, I subconsciously felt a presence around me. I had my knife on my left side where she was standing. She had come back and asked me if she could lay down. It was a bit chilly and she was getting cold and probably tired of wandering around aimlessly with only a T-shirt on. She asked me where she could defecate. I handed her some paper tissues and told her to go by the bridge. After she relieved herself, she laid by my side and I extended my cover to her. When I woke up later around 5:00 am, she was not there. Like a ghost, she simply had disappeared the same way she had appeared. Hopefully she had come to her senses and returned home.

THE HOMELESS DUDE WHO POSTED PORNOGRAPHIC PICTURES ON HIS SHIRT:

I was at MacPherson Park one Sunday and attended Church service led by a Korean pastor who serves meals to the homeless after preaching to them every Sunday at the park. He and his folks brought and set up chairs for the homeless to sit and a podium from where he preached and had people playing instruments. When he invited anyone who had a prayer request to step up to the podium so that he would pray for them, a homeless guy walked to him with a large and noticeable pornographic picture of a naked woman, stuck to his side. It was unbelievable that this dude did not care that there were in attendance, children, parents and church members who were there to serve the homeless.

Everybody was stupefied but nobody rebuked him. Even the pastor and his assistants feigned not to see the image while they laid their hand on him and prayed for him. I tried in vain to tell him to take off the picture and even attempted to snatch it but he simply ignored me. I saw him at the Mc Kenna Center few days later. He stood in the line for dinner and had another but smaller and almost unnoticeable image of a naked woman on his side, unlike the one in the park which was visible from afar. I thought about saying something but left it alone and simply hoped that the young men and the older folks who were serving the meals as volunteers would not see the irreverent image. One morning, I got to the center at about 8:30 am and walked to the line for breakfast which is served there from 8:00 am to 9:00

am. I and another person who had just got there tried to get in front of those who were in the line for the second time, after they had already got served. All of them acquiesced to let us cut in front of them, but the same guy who had the pornographic picture in the park objected when I walked in front of him. "Man, I'm first time. You already had breakfast," I told him. "I don't care if it is your first time," he answered. I was offended and retorted "I don't care if you want to get breakfast for a second time either." "If you don't care about somebody having breakfast for the first time, why you think I should care about you trying to eat twice?" I added.

Another day, he was back in the line for breakfast and I was behind him this time. He got some coffee, from one of the old folks who were volunteering to serve breakfast. When the next volunteer who served the pastries asked him which one he wanted, he spitefully and callously responded "I don't want that nasty shit."

I just could not understand, how a homeless person who relied on charitable assistance and services, could be so mean, rude and ungrateful to people who were benevolently devoted to volunteer their time to help, assist and serve him. I had not gone to the center for a month, but I have not seen him around since I returned there, until now. Had he been barred from the place? I can't tell. Whether he left town, got jailed or died, I can't tell. But he is the kind of despicable creature who makes people not feel sorry for the homeless.

CHRONIC HOMELESS WHO GET FREE HOUSING BUT PREFER TO SLEEP OUTSIDE:

A chronic homeless man, who I will identify as A, informed me that he was in the process of getting an apartment through social service assistance. Two weeks later, I was in a park late at night when he walked though and told me that he had finally got a place in South East, Washington DC. I was so happy for him because he had lived on the streets for decades and was now fortunate enough to have a place to call home. One Friday night, less than a week after he got his place, I saw him walking through the same park and he stopped to talk to me. He told me that he had just got off the train at the Gallery place Metro station, and was on his way to panhandle by the clubs on K Street in downtown.

I found it odd that he was carrying several bags. "Why are you carrying all these bags?" I asked him. "Oh, I am staying out for the week-end and I will be panhandling all day, so I brought some stuff to change clothes." I did not understand why he wanted to sleep out on the street even for a week-end, although I understood clearly that he was going to be making money and indulge in his drug habits on week-end nights, when the streets were crowded with people going to party at the numerous clubs in the vicinity. "But you can panhandling and enjoy yourself all night and go back to your apartment in the morning, and then, come back in the evening. You don't have to sleep outside anymore, I told him." But he insisted that, he wanted to spend the week-end outside and return home on Sunday. A week later, I found out that he never went back to his apartment and had been sleeping every night outside around the McPherson metro station. I waited another week and walked up to the station and there he was, lying on the ground by the entrance of the metro station and shivering under a blanket, while the temperature was below the freezing point.

I got very incensed to see him freeze under a blanket outside in the middle of the cold night, while he had a fully furnished one bedroom apartment with a flat screen TV and the rent and all the bills, paid for him.

"Leo you don't understand he told me. I just get bored staying in the apartment by myself. I have been sleeping on the streets for more than 10 years, and I feel more comfortable out here, than staying inside all day. It is just depressing to me, to stay inside." He told me. "But you got to make yourself get used to it. You don't have to stay in all day. Actually, you can come out and stay out all day, but every night, you have to go in, so that you can get used to sleeping inside." I replied to him. But my plea to him to give himself a chance by going to his apartment regularly until he gets acclimated to staying indoors, fell on deaf ears.

A homeless couple who were smoking crack with him outside moved themselves in to his apartment, while he kept sleeping outside every night and rarely went home. But, since he had a crack habit, the lady crackhead who had moved herself in his apartment found some crack dealers in the neighborhood who used to come and serve her in the apartment, when he returned home with money from panhandling. I guess staying home was no longer boring because he had people to keep him company. He finally got used to going back home after panhandling downtown and no longer sleeps outside. The lady has been staying with him since, but her boyfriend, who initially took her there, moved out.

This story is not unique. Here is the case of another homeless man, who I will identify as R. He also has got a free fully-furnished apartment more than five years ago. But up to this day, he never spent a full day inside. No matter how cold the winter, or hot the summer, he sleeps every night on a bench at the McPherson Park or on the ground on the White House side of McPherson Metro station. As in the previous case, he also allowed a homeless couple to move in his apartment, but he has been sleeping outside. Ultimately the social worker on his case had the couple move out, and helped them get their own free apartment because they were chronic homeless also. He was moved to a new apartment, but he still sleeps outside. When I asked him who was staying in his apartment, he told me, his brother.

There is also the case of another chronic homeless who I will identify as J. He invited his homeless buddies to move in with him when he got his free furnished apartment. But although he initially had two friends move in, his place ended up being infested with almost four to five more of his homeless buddies, including a couple. One night, I saw him standing in the freezing cold outside a Mac Donald in Chinatown and asked him why he did not go home. He answered that too many people had invaded his apartment and he was not comfortable staying in with the crowd. In other words, he was scared to go home to his own apartment because of some of the guys who were staying in there, and were running the place and even engaging in illegal activities in there. "Why don't you get your case manager, to move them out?" I suggested to him. He said his social worker had been to the apartment on several occasions and asked the extra occupants to leave, but none of them moved out. He later got jailed for something that I do not remember. While he was in jail for few months, one of the guys sold all the furniture and appliances in the apartment. When I saw him after he was released, he got another apartment for free again, and repeated the very same mistakes by inviting his homeless friends from the streets to move in. The last time I heard about him, I was told that the only person who was staying with him was a lady from the homeless shelter who moved in with him, and that she had a lot of control over him. She probably successfully got everybody else out of there and made him comfortable to stay in his own apartment. The last time I had seen him, he told me that he was taking his medications and was visiting his psychiatrist regularly. I have not seen him on the streets since. I guess he had been staying inside his apartment frequently because he found the right company and had been getting some psychiatric help.

I also have some sad stories to tell, such as the case of Franck. He was the prototypical chronic homeless. He has been living on the street for over 20 years without interruption, except the numerous times he had recurrently spent behind bars. He was a trouble maker and occasionally a bully who preyed on the weak on the streets and took from them, when he could successfully intimidate them. Obviously, he suffered from mental illness and drug addiction, but he was just a normal person surviving on the streets. One day, I saw him in Chinatown after he had just left the hospital and got off the bus while still wearing the hospital gown. "What happened to you?" I asked him. He told me that a couple of nights before, when he was in the back alley, a young street hustler walked back there and distributed little pieces of crack cocaine to those who were back there smocking crack and asked them to let him know about the quality of his product. Many of the youngsters who were selling crack in the area were competing against one another, and whoever had the best product was attracting more customers. When the young dude came back to the alley few minutes later to inquire about the quality of his product, Franck simply responded "your shit is garbage-meaning that the crack was not potent, therefore not good-. The young hustler, could not digest the truth from Franck's mouth. He pulled a knife and stabbed Franck in the stomach. But Franck, who was about 6 foot 3 tall and weighed about 250 pounds, survived the stab wounds and left the hospital before the doctor released him.

He was a man in his 40s, whose entire adult life was spent on the streets as a homeless, in jails as recidivist, in hospital's emergency rooms as frequent patient and victim of crime. I could therefore imagine and feel his happiness, when I run through him one day and he told me, with excitement, that he had been told that a social worker had come in the alley to let him know that he had got a place. When I saw him the next day, he told me that he had talked to the social worker and that he was going to get the keys of his apartment the following day. Unfortunately, two days later, someone told me that Franck had been struck by a truck while he was crossing the street and died on the scene of the accident. This was one of the unhappiest news I ever heard. A man, who had been homeless for most of his adult life, gets killed as soon as he finally get a place that he never had a chance to move in. I was saddened.

CHAPTER 7:

FACTS ON HOMELESSNESS

It was never my intention to write a research book on homelessness but to only explain my own experience with homelessness. Before I conclude the book, I want to share some basic facts about homelessness in America from various sources posted online. Hopefully this will help the reader get informed and realize how serious a problem homelessness is and who is affected by it. I seriously consider becoming a homeless activist myself when I am no longer homeless. Then, I would devote some time to do my own research and collection of facts by visiting homeless communities in other parts of the US. But now, I can only present these few facts from other sources.

GENERAL HOMELESS FACTS: (From Greendoors.com)

<u>What does "homeless" mean?</u>

The Department of Housing and Urban Development defines homelessness in four broad categories:

• People who are living in a place not meant for human habitation, in emergency shelter, in transitional housing, or are exiting an institution where they temporarily resided.

• People who are losing their primary nighttime residence, which may include a motel or hotel or a doubled up situation, within 14 days and lack resources or support networks to remain in housing.

• Families with children or unaccompanied youth who are unstably housed and likely to continue in that state.

• People who are fleeing or attempting to flee domestic violence, have no other residence, and lack the resources or support networks to obtain other permanent housing.

<u>Who is at risk of homelessness?</u>

The face of homelessness is changing. Though veterans, people with disabilities, and single parent families have always been at high-risk for homelessness, today, more and more of our country's working poor are struggling with or at risk of homelessness. People recently released from prison and young adults who have recently been emancipated (or aged-out) from the foster care system are also at increased risk of homelessness. And, in Central Texas, the fastest growing homeless population is women and children.

What does it mean to be "chronically homeless?"

A "chronically homeless" person is defined as "an unaccompanied homeless individual with a disabling condition who has either been continuously homeless for a year or more, or has had at least four episodes of homelessness in the past three years."

Although chronic homelessness represents a small share of the overall homeless population (approximately 123,790 chronically homeless individuals nationwide on any given night), chronically homeless people use up a significantly disproportionate share of the services. Many chronically homeless people have a serious mental illness like schizophrenia and/or an alcohol or drug addiction.

What does doubled-up mean?

Doubled-up refers to people who live with friends, family or other nonrelatives for economic reasons. This population has been steadily rising in recent years, having increased by more than 50% from 2005 to 2010. In 2010, it was estimated that 6.8 million people were living doubled-up. (Source: http://www.greendoors.org/facts/general-data.php)

10 FACTS ABOUT HOMELESSNESS: (From, *Huffington Post*)

Fact 1: Over half a million people are homeless. On any given night, there are over 600,000 homeless people in the U.S., according to the US Department of Housing and Urban Development (HUD). Most people are spending the night either in homeless shelters or in some sort of short-term transitional housing. Slightly more than a third are living in cars or under bridges or are in some other way living unsheltered.

Fact 2: One quarter of homeless people are children. HUD reports that on any given night, over 138,000 of the homeless in the U.S. are children under the age of 18. Thousands of these homeless children are unaccompanied, according to HUD. Another federal program, No Child Left Behind, defines "homeless children" more broadly and includes not just those living in shelters or transitional housing but those who are sharing the housing of other persons due to economic hardship; living in cars, parks, bus or train stations; or awaiting foster-care placement. Under this definition, the National Center for Homeless Education reported in September 2014 that local school districts reported there are over 1 million homeless children in public schools.

Fact 3: Tens of thousands of veterans are homeless. Over 57,000 veterans are homeless each night, according to HUD. Sixty percent of them are in shelters, the rest unsheltered. Nearly 5,000 are female.

Fact 4: Domestic violence is a leading cause of homelessness among women. According to the National Law Center on Homelessness and Poverty (NLCHP), more than 90 percent of homeless women are victims of severe physical or sexual abuse, and escaping that abuse is a leading cause of their homelessness.

Fact 5: Many people are homeless because they cannot afford rent. The lack of affordable housing is a primary cause of homelessness, according to the NLCHP. HUD has seen its budget slashed by over 50 percent in recent decades, resulting in the loss of 10,000 units of subsidized low-income housing each and every year.

Fact 6: There are fewer places for poor people to rent than before. According to the NLCHP, one eighth of the nation's supply of low-income housing has been permanently lost since 2001. The U.S. needs at least 7 million more affordable apartments for low-income families, and as a result, millions of families spend more than half of their monthly income on rent.

Fact 7: In the last few years millions have lost their homes. Over 5 million homes have been foreclosed on since 2008; that's one out of every 10 homes with a mortgage. This has caused even more people to search for affordable rental property.

Fact 8: The government does not help as much as you think. There is enough public rental assistance to help about one out of every four extremely low-income households. Those who do not receive help are on multi-year waiting lists. For example, Charlotte just opened up their applications for public housing assistance for the first time in 14 years, and over 10,000 people applied.

Fact 9: One in five homeless people suffers from untreated severe mental illness. While about 6 percent of the general population suffers from severe mental illness, 20 to 25 percent of the homeless suffer from severe mental illness, according to government studies. Half of this population self-medicate and are at further risk for addiction and poor physical health. A University of Pennsylvania study tracking nearly 5,000 homeless people for two years discovered that investing in comprehensive health support and treatment of physical and mental illnesses is less costly than incarceration, shelter and hospital services for the untreated homeless.

Fact 10: Cities are increasingly making homelessness a crime. A 2014 survey of 187 cities by the NLCHP found that 24 percent of cities make it a city-wide crime to beg in public, 33 percent make it illegal to stand around or loiter anyplace in the city, 18 percent make it a crime to sleep anywhere in public, 43 percent make it illegal to sleep in your car, and 53 percent make it illegal to sit or lie down in particular public places. And the number of cities criminalizing homelessness is steadily increasing.

Source: http://www.huffingtonpost.com/bill-quigley/tenfacts-about-homelessn_b_5977946.html

CHAPTER 8:

CAN HOMELESSNESS BE SOLVED?

I was sitting on the corner of 14th and G Streets when a middle-aged white man dressed in dark suit and tie walked by and stopped to chat with me. He told me, that he was a social scientist and was politically active against poverty. "How are we going to end this?" He said to me, in reference to homelessness. He confided to me that in his professional life- without telling me precisely what his profession was- he was very committed to fight to end homelessness, and despite all efforts and ideas he could come up with, he was very pessimistic that such a battle could be won. He had a very despondent look on his face.

If a person, who has an educational and professional background in the field of social science, and who focuses on ending homelessness, finds it hard to come up with a solution, it would be arrogant of me, to pretend that I know how to end homelessness in America. So, I can only share my humble inexpert opinion which is that a solution to homelessness must come from the system, the community and the individual homeless themselves. Here is what I suggest:

THE INDIVIDUAL:

The brightest minds can theorize all kinds of solutions to end homelessness, but the homeless individuals are the ones who should be concerned more than anybody else, about ending their predicament by all means necessary. They should not be content with their status but instead do whatever it takes to get out of it. They have to figure out what to do to improve their condition, seek and take advantage of the help and services available out there to sustain themselves daily and most importantly, make moves to become stable and end their homelessness. A homeless person who tries hard enough can find help to feed himself daily, have a temporary roof over his head, receive free medical, mental health and legal assistance, free clothes and every other help, to address his or her urgent basic needs. But even with the abundance of help, a homeless man or woman may remain homeless on a chronic base, if he or she, becomes too reliant on charity, instead of seeking to become independent.

-Nobody can survive without food, and a person who is not properly nourished cannot function properly. The government of the city of Washington D.C, provides food stamps to the homeless residents of the District of Columbia. But those who do not qualify for food stamps for whatever reasons or have no means to feed themselves, must seek and find places, where free food is served. I don't know about other states, but in Washington D.C, a homeless person cannot go hungry if he or she makes the effort to find, and go to soup kitchens, churches and food truck where breakfast, lunch or dinner are served daily and all year long, in and around the downtown area and surrounding neighborhoods. Any homeless man or woman who goes to bed hungry in Washington D.C is simply lazy, or unwilling to make the effort to go and get some free food available all over the city. A homeless person who does not have to worry about food can at least focus on doing other things to improve their condition and save money that can be used for transportation to go and seek a job or take care of other urgent needs.

-A person who does not have adequate sleep and rest, will not be able to function properly. In most cities, like here in Washington D.C, there are homeless shelters available for men, women and families, although most of them are overnight shelters, where the homeless have to check-in in the evening, and check-out early in the morning. There are also opportunity for low-income housing assistance from the government and charitable organizations for the homeless who have a mental or physical disability, are single mothers or are veterans of the US armed forces. Some organizations also help the chronic homeless get free or affordable housing, for those who receive some income from government assistance or no income at all. Unfortunately, many homeless who qualify for low-income housing assistance do not bother to apply for them, and those who do, have to wait sometimes for too long before the government provides them housing. I will advise the homeless who do not like to go to shelters or do not qualify for housing assistance, to get some money by working a day job or panhandling and use it to purchase a tent and find a place where to set it up. I know it is easier said than done, because the city's authorities do not allow camping on public sites. But that is exactly what I did. Sometimes, a homeless person has to do what he has to do to survive. I have been in my tent for at least two years, despite the threats by the city's authorities to remove it. Now, I am working towards earning enough to afford a place to live. But the tent has helped me a whole lot because, at least, I had a place to keep my belongings and take care of myself. I could not do so if I was sleeping in a shelter every night and checking out every morning without being able to secure my belongings.

A homeless man who sleeps outside can still take care of his or her hygiene because there are several places, at least in the city of Washington D.C, where a homeless man or woman can go and shower every day. There are also places where a homeless person can get free clothes. There is therefore no excuse for a homeless man or woman to be filthy. A homeless man or woman who wants to get a job, cannot go to a job interview with dirty clothes and a poor hygiene. It is therefore important for a person who wants to end his homeless condition to take care of his hygiene, so that he or she can be presentable when opportunities show up.

-A homeless person who has a mental or physical illness should seek help because, if he or she is not addressing his or her health issues, very likely he or she will remain homeless. A person who is diagnosed with a mental or physical disability is eligible to receive social assistance from the government. Many mentally and physically disabled homeless are receiving housing assistance. But there are still many homeless men and women on the streets who are not applying for social assistance as they should.

Here in Washington D.C, homeless individuals who are citizens and legal residents of the U.S, have access to free healthcare. The Homeless who are in need of medical care must get free assurance and go the free clinics available to them. Those who can't, must go to the emergency room of any hospital if they have an urgent medical need, because they won't be denied medical emergency attention.

A person who has no money cannot afford anything; and a person who is not employed cannot legally earn enough money to afford a roof over his head. A homeless person who is able to legally work in the US should not give up on seeking employment, although it is not evident that he or she will find a job. It is obvious that there are not enough jobs in the U.S, for everybody who needs one. But there are people who are not working because they are not looking for a job; or when they get a job, they do not keep it. In Washington D.C, there are also many day labor agencies which pay minimum wage or a little less. Although it is not a secured and reliable employment, day labor can help homeless men and women earn some money and save most of it, while they are staying at shelters or camping outside and getting meals at soup kitchens or food trucks. Also, a homeless man or woman who is not employed must also consider being an entrepreneur, and start a small legal lucrative business activity. Although in Washington D.C vending without license is illegal, I have seen some homeless men and women vend oils, umbrellas or clothes as ambulant vendors. I do not know the conditions and requirements to obtain a vending license, but homeless street vendors can find a way to obtain their vending license and make money on the streets. What I am basically saying is that, a homeless person should always try to earn some means, and not simply accept to remain destitute and rely on handouts.

Even if a person has to beg to have something rather than nothing, I think he or she should put their pride aside and do so. Although panhandling is seen as degrading and shameful, it is legal here in Washington D.C, and many homeless make a lot of money panhandling. Here are the conditions under which panhandling are permitted or not permitted in the District of Columbia:

"Panhandling (often soliciting for money) is not illegal on public space unless it is done in an aggressive manner or at/near certain locations. No person, for example, can ask, beg or solicit alms within 10 feet of an automated teller machine (ATM), or on buses or the Metro and at bus, subway or train stops and stations. Soliciting also is unacceptable in other instances, such as in exchange for cleaning motor vehicle windows while the vehicle is in traffic on a public street and on private property or residential property, without permission from the owner

or occupant. Aggressive panhandling on public space is illegal. It is considered aggressive when accompanied by one or more of the following acts: Approaching, speaking to or following a person in a way that would cause a reasonable person to fear bodily harm or the commission of a crime; Touching a person in the course of soliciting without that person's consent; Continuously soliciting from or following a person after the person has made a negative response; Intentionally blocking or interfering with the safe passage of a person or a vehicle; and Acting with the intent of intimidating another person into giving money or another thing of value."

Regardless of those who may make a moral issue of it, panhandling is legal here in Washington D.C, which means that it is ok for a homeless person to beg, if he or she has to. The problem is not whether a person panhandles or not, but what he or she does with the money. As long as he or she uses the money to take care of urgent needs and do not make of panhandling a profession, I think he or she should, instead of having nothing at all. I acknowledge that it takes humility and strength to convince oneself to beg because the average person will not do it because of pride. I had to put my pride aside, be strong and humble myself to beg. I have been able to write and print this book because I panhandled and used the money to purchase a brand new laptop on sale for $499. If I had to worry about what somebody else thought about me begging, I would have not been able to purchase this computer and write this book.

Many homeless who are not able to work because of physical and mental health issues are legally considered disabled and entitled to a monthly disability social security assistance payment from the government. Those who have a disability but are not getting a monthly disability check from the government, should make the effort to get it because they are entitled to it. And they should use the money to pay rent.

And last but the least, the Homeless who have legal issues, must seek free legal help which is available here in Washington D.C and other parts of the country.

To sum it up, whatever the issue is that causes a person to be and stay homeless, he or she has to be humble enough to acknowledge his or her problem, seek help and assistance, and take the necessary actions to end their homelessness.

THE SYSTEM:

Travelers from other wealthy developed nations who come to the United States are shocked when they see so many homeless individuals in the streets of major cities of the world's wealthiest and mightiest country.

Many of the world wealthiest capitalist nations do not have an acute homeless problem like in the U.S, because their governments have social programs to assist and provide for the welfare of the needy and poorest in their society. This is true for nations like; Germany, Sweden, France, Denmark, The Netherlands or Switzerland, in Europe; Japan, South Korea, Singapore, Australia or New Zealand, in South Asia and the Pacific ocean; and Israel, Qatar, Bahrain and Saudi Arabia in the Middle East.

In America, the very idea of government providing assistance or welfare to the poor and the most vulnerable of society is considered socialism. Socialism is vehemently opposed and barely tolerated by the conservative and liberal sides of the American political spectrum. To make it simple, in America, the common reasoning in defense of capitalism and in opposition to socialism is that; it is not the role of the government to do for people what they are able to do for themselves if they are willing to work hard and take advantage of the opportunities offered by free market economy and the freedoms and liberties guaranteed in the U.S Constitution. Those who fail to achieve economic and social stability but end up in poverty and homelessness are held responsible for their own misery. Consequently, the solution to better their condition is expected of the individuals and not the government.

Because of her wealth, might and freedoms, America is indeed a land of opportunity and attracts people from around the globe. They come here legally and illegally with the hope of achieving prosperity for themselves and their families. The success stories of those who came here with nothing, took advantage of opportunities, worked hard or started a business and ended up achieving success and prosperity are innumerable.

I will give a simple example. From 1974 to1991, a civil war in Ethiopia resulted in the death of 1.4 million Ethiopians. Images of millions of starving Ethiopians were broadcast on television screens all over the world. Many Ethiopians who lost everything in their country were given visas to migrate to the U.S. Many of them migrated to the Washington D.C area and took advantage of their newly found liberty and opportunities of free market, to organize themselves and start small businesses. These Ethiopian migrants who left their war ravaged country with nothing, own a plethora of businesses including gas stations, dollar stores and Ethiopian Restaurants, in the affluent neighborhoods of Adams Morgan and U Street and elsewhere all over the greater Washington DC region today.

Such success stories inhibit Americans' empathy for the poor or homeless because it is presumed that anybody who tries hard enough can make it. Therefore, poverty and homelessness are no excuses for reliance on government assistance and relief, because the same opportunities to make it are supposed to exist for everybody in this democratic free market capitalist system.

So I don't know how homelessness can be eradicated in America unless the system is reformed. I can only hope that some geniuses will figure out how to end homelessness in America without any reform to the system.

The phenomenon of widespread homelessness has its roots in social issues and political decisions that affected the community as a whole. About 10 years ago, policy decisions resulted into the closure of mental institutions across the USA like the Saint Elizabeth Hospital in Washington D.C. As a consequence, thousands of mentally-ill individuals who constitute the majority of the homeless, were released on the streets of Washington D.C and other urban and rural areas all across America. One solution to drastically reduce the number of the homeless on the streets is for the powers-that-be to get off the streets, the mentally-ill homeless and help them with housing or shelters where they can receive assistance, treatment and care. Because of mental illnesses, substance abuse, physical ailments or a history of abuse, many homeless men and women, who have the greatest needs for services, do not access them. There is therefore a need to find those homeless in need of service and connect them to the service they need.

Wages that helped people obtain and keep their houses have been declining because of the relocation of jobs out of the country by corporations who seek to hire cheap labor overseas in order to maximize their profits. The advance of technologies have also caused hundreds of thousands of workers in the US to lose their jobs. For example, today, there are self-checking machines which have replaced workers in groceries stores like CVS. It is easy to accuse the homeless of not wanting to work. But, the reality is that there are not enough jobs available to remedy the problem of unemployment in the U.S. To create enough jobs for everybody including the homeless and reduce homelessness in America, the legislative and executive branches of power in the U.S, must take actions to force U.S corporations and companies to move the jobs back to the U.S from China and other places in Asia and Latin America where they manufacture most of their goods by hiring cheap labor there.

Also, while executives of big businesses are taking huge salaries home, the average worker who earns minimum wage and works full-time, is still not making enough to lift himself out of poverty. Many workers have to work extra jobs to make ends meet. Many homeless do work full time on minimum wage but are not earning enough to pay rent, because in many urban areas like in Washington D.C, minimum wage is lower than living wage. The solution to end homelessness for many homeless workers is therefore that the politicians increase minimum wage and make it equal to living wage.

It is true that many individuals end up and stay homeless as a result of drug addiction and it is fair to hold them responsible for their choice to do drugs. But, it is also a fact that the drug addiction epidemic in America is the result of proliferation of highly addictive and very cheap street drugs like crack cocaine, heroin, crystal meth and synthetic drugs. It cost billions and more to the government to arrest and jail homeless people over drug offenses and treat them in emergency rooms. That money should instead be used for drug rehabilitation and treatment and housing for those homeless addicts.

It is a shame that many homeless men are veterans who have served in the U.S armed forces and fought on war battlefields abroad. The U.S government must provide housing to all homeless veterans   and treat those suffering from mental illnesses, post traumatic syndromes, drug addiction and other psychological and psychiatric disorders.

Homelessness is also caused by high cost of housing, especially in urban areas where low income people simply cannot afford to pay their rent. Homelessness can be alleviated by creating the conditions for the development of sufficient low income housing in urban areas where so many low income people work and live.

So many people who are released from Jail, prisons and foster cares are discharged into homelessness.

I can go on and on, but most experts, professionals, social workers and activists agree about the most effective way to solve homelessness. They propose that: Actions and services must be coordinated as a complex machine from the state level to the local non-profit organization. And all agencies helping with Housing, substance abuse detoxification and treatment, clinics for health, mental illness, substance abuse, emergency shelter and services should work together as one organism to meet the complex need of each homeless. If one agency tries to do it alone, it will be very difficult to meet that complex need. But, most importantly, as one specialist suggested; it all boils down to people helping people. Human beings working with other human beings to build trust, find the root problem of their issue and develop specialized individual plans for that person.

THE COMMUNITY:

The solutions to homelessness- which has reached an epidemic proportion in America- cannot only come from the government, charitable organizations and the individual themselves. The community must also be involved. By community, I mean everybody who is not directly affected by homelessness and who may not feel concerned by it.

It blows my mind how people see thousands of their fellow human beings sleeping on the street and live in total destitution in the midst of plenty and do not feel outraged by it. It amazes me how people are so involved with advocating, rallying and marching for gay rights, animal rights, protection of the environment, guns right, abortion and anti-abortion issues, police brutality, immigration issues, opposition to or support for foreign wars, rights of minority groups, health related issues (cure for cancer, Aids etc.), religious and other political and social issues, but when it comes to homelessness, I do not see the same public passion, outrage and mobilization to demand an end to homelessness.

You, whoever you are, must stop shaming and blaming the homeless and instead help them restore their dignity with; a smile, a hand shake, a look into their eyes instead of ignoring their presence, a brief conversation to offer them words of hope and encouragement. Even though your compassion and respect for a homeless person will not suffice to end his or her predicament, at least it will create the consciousness in you to support efforts to end homelessness.

I would like to see millions of people gathering on the national mall in Washington D.C one day, to demand an end to homelessness. I would like to see a public outcry and pressure on politicians and the government to demand actions to end the epidemic of homelessness in America.

It is only when the people will rise and demand that their government make of homelessness an emergency and a priority that the politicians and decision makers, will seriously focus on solving the homelessness plague. The people must therefore mobilize and, like other organizations who are very vocal about their issues, tell the powers-that-be that, homeless lives matter!